Ext JS Data-driven Application Design

A step-by-step guide to building a user-friendly database
in Ext JS using data from an existing database

Kazuhiro Kotsutsumi

[PACKT] open source *

PUBLISHING

community experience distilled

BIRMINGHAM - MUMBAI

Ext JS Data-driven Application Design

First published: December 2013

Production Reference: 1171213

Published by Packt Publishing Ltd.
Livery Place
35 Livery Street
Birmingham B3 2PB, UK.

ISBN 978-1-78216-544-6

www.packtpub.com

Cover Image by Tom Coulton (tom.coulton@xenophy.com)

Credits

Author
Kazuhiro Kotsutsumi

Reviewers
Gagandeep Singh
Adrian Teodorescu
Li Xudong

Acquisition Editor
Joanne Fitzpatrick

Commissioning Editors
Llewellyn Rozario
Deepika Singh

Technical Editors
Rosmy George
Manal Pednekar
Veena Pagare

Project Coordinator
Akash Poojary

Copy Editors
Alisha Aranha
Roshni Banerjee
Mradula Hegde
Gladson Monteiro
Deepa Nambiar
Laxmi Subramanian

Proofreader
Lucy Rowland

Indexer
Hemangini Bari

Production Coordinator
Kyle Albuquerque

Cover Work
Kyle Albuquerque

Foreword

Ext JS Data-driven Application Design, by *Kazuhiro Kotsutsumi*, is a practical hands-on guide for both intermediate and expert JavaScript developers using Sencha's Ext JS 4.x framework.

This book is aimed at developers who not only want to learn how to develop a real-life desktop application that can read from and write to a database, but also want to see how to use the framework's advanced features they might not yet have heard of.

Kazuhiro begins describing the application development process by leading the reader through the database structure that the application will be using.

He continues by laying out the application structure using the MCV (model-view-controller) pattern — decoupling the UI, data, and business-logic — while detailing how to use Sencha's CLI tool Sencha CMD (Sencha Command) to help in that process.

He utilizes the framework's power by showing the reader how to use the advanced feature Ext Direct, describing in detail and with code examples what it is, how to add it, and how to use it in an application. He also brings in browser history support and again points out clearly how and why it can be used in an application.

Finally, after describing how to add and read database entries into the application and back to the server, he finishes his book explaining how to visualize the data in different charts and importing to or exporting from the database.

By using the carefully described features introduced in this book, you too can use this great architecture to build your own future applications.

Stefan Stölzle

Sr. Solutions Engineer - Professional Services

Sencha, Inc.

www.sencha.com

About the Author

Kazuhiro Kotsutsumi was born in Sapporo, Japan in 1979. He started using C/C++ at the age of 14 and proceeded to learn MASM, Delphi, ActionScript, PHP, C#, Perl, and so on.

After working for a web systems development company while enrolled at college, he began programming built-in functions for cell phones.

Having worked as a Project Manager and a freelance programmer for one year, he established his company Xenophy CO., LTD in 2006.

Xenophy has always offered a variety of IT web solutions and has become synonymous with the promotion and expansion of Sencha in Japan.

Currently, Xenophy is a Sencha Reseller and the official Sencha training partner in Japan. In September 2013, Xenophy announced the launch of Sencha Official Training in Japan, a fully localized course with Sencha's official training materials adapted for the Japanese market.

He has already published two Sencha Ext JS guides in Japanese, including *Sencha EXT JS 4 – A Practical Developing Guide* and he recently co-authored a Sencha Touch guide.

I would like to thank Yuuya Tanaka, Kazuhiro Yasunaga, Hisashi Nakamura, and Tom Miyagawa Coulton for making this book possible with their hard work and help.

About the Reviewers

Gagandeep Singh is a Software Engineer with five years' experience in distributed systems and data-driven web application development. He has expertise in Java and JavaScript. He holds a Master's degree in Computer Science from the University of Florida.

He started his career with Infosys, then moved on to Siemens Research, and is now working with WalmartLabs.

Adrian Teodorescu is a professional software developer who has been working with Sencha's frameworks since 2009. He has developed plugins, extensions, and apps with both Ext JS and Sencha Touch. You can check out some of his work on his website at www.mzsolutions.eu.

Li Xudong is a frontend developer in Beijing, China. He is skilled in JavaScript, CSS, HTML, node.js, and Python, and wants to make things better.

www.PacktPub.com

Support files, eBooks, discount offers and more

You might want to visit www.PacktPub.com for support files and downloads related to your book.

Did you know that Packt offers eBook versions of every book published, with PDF and ePub files available? You can upgrade to the eBook version at www.PacktPub.com and as a print book customer, you are entitled to a discount on the eBook copy. Get in touch with us at service@packtpub.com for more details.

At www.PacktPub.com, you can also read a collection of free technical articles, sign up for a range of free newsletters and receive exclusive discounts and offers on Packt books and eBooks.

http://PacktLib.PacktPub.com

Do you need instant solutions to your IT questions? PacktLib is Packt's online digital book library. Here, you can access, read and search across Packt's entire library of books.

Why Subscribe?
- Fully searchable across every book published by Packt
- Copy and paste, print and bookmark content
- On demand and accessible via web browser

Free Access for Packt account holders

If you have an account with Packt at www.PacktPub.com, you can use this to access PacktLib today and view nine entirely free books. Simply use your login credentials for immediate access.

Table of Contents

Preface

Ext JS is a leading JavaScript framework that comes with a wealth of components, APIs, and extensive documentation that you can harness to build powerful and interactive desktop applications. By using Ext JS, you also quickly develop rich desktop web applications that are compatible with all major browsers. This book will take you step-by-step through building a clear and user-friendly sales database in Ext JS using information from an existing database.

Rather than just explaining MVC, this book is a hands-on, practical guide that will take you through the mechanics of building an application. By the end of the book you will have a working application that is ready to customize. You can also use the architecture from this book in future projects to simplify controls, improve maintenance, and expand applications with ease.

You should be able to grasp the idea of the example data structure introduced in this book. This book has been written on the premise that you are familiar with JavaScript and have basic operational knowledge of MySQL.

What this book covers

Chapter 1, Data Structure, focuses on preparing the basic foundations of your database. It will deal with an existing virtual company's data structure and the making of SQL and tables in MySQL.

Chapter 2, Planning Application Design, develops the environment of the project, while at the same time introducing Sencha Cmd. You will learn to design a simple application and optimize Ajax requests in order to use Ext Direct and Ext.util.History to control the screen with a URL.

Chapter 3, Data Input, discusses making a form to input data, then transmit that data to a server via Ext Direct. You will also learn to monitor the state of the input and how Ext Direct will validate it on the server side.

Chapter 4, List and Search, speaks mainly about displaying data that we read in *Chapter 3, Data Input*. However, users will no doubt want to search the data, so this chapter will also introduce data searches.

Chapter 5, Reporting, focuses on the implementation of the report displaying it with four different types of graphs on the dashboard.

Chapter 6, Data Management, focuses on the implementation of data import/export, done to restore or to keep a backup of the data.

What you need for this book

For using this book, you will need to be familiar with JavaScript and have a basic operational knowledge of MySQL.

Before you start reading, you need to have the following setup in your system:

- The most recent version of Sencha Ext JS with GPL. You can download this from the Sencha website available at `http://www.sencha.com/products/extjs/download/`. This book was made based on Ext JS Version 4.2.2.
- Any good code editor.
- A web browser, any modern web browser is okay. In this book we are using Google Chrome, so we suggest that you use Google Chrome as well, if possible.

Who this book is for

This is a tutorial for intermediates in Sencha Ext JS that explains the process of building a UI that deals with an existing database.

This book is for anyone who wants to be able to systematically learn how to construct an application from the first step of implementation.

Conventions

In this book, you will find a number of styles of text that distinguish between different kinds of information. Here are some examples of these styles, and an explanation of their meaning.

Code words in text are shown as follows: "The `Bill` table is almost the same as the `Quotation` table."

A block of code is set as follows:

```
UPDATE
    users
SET
    email='extkazuhiro@xenophy.com',
    passwd=SHA1(MD5('password')),
    lastname='Kotsutsumi',
    firstname='Kazuhiro',
    modified=NOW()
WHERE
    id=1
```

Any command-line input or output is written as follows:

```
# The name of the package containing the theme scss for the app
app.theme=ext-theme-classic
↓
# The name of the package containing the theme scss for the app
app.theme=ext-theme-neptune
```

New terms and **important words** are shown in bold. Words that you see on the screen, in menus or dialog boxes for example, appear in the text like this: "By doing this, you can keep deleting just by continuing to click on the **Delete** button."

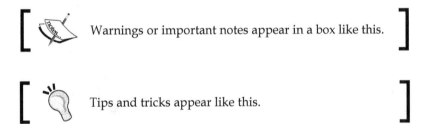

Warnings or important notes appear in a box like this.

Tips and tricks appear like this.

Reader feedback

Feedback from our readers is always welcome. Let us know what you think about this book—what you liked or may have disliked. Reader feedback is important for us to develop titles that you really get the most out of.

To send us general feedback, simply send an e-mail to feedback@packtpub.com, and mention the book title via the subject of your message.

If there is a topic that you have expertise in and you are interested in either writing or contributing to a book, see our author guide on www.packtpub.com/authors.

Customer support

Now that you are the proud owner of a Packt book, we have a number of things to help you to get the most from your purchase.

Downloading the example code

You can download the example code files for all Packt books you have purchased from your account at `http://www.packtpub.com`. If you purchased this book elsewhere, you can visit `http://www.packtpub.com/support` and register to have the files e-mailed directly to you.

Errata

Although we have taken every care to ensure the accuracy of our content, mistakes do happen. If you find a mistake in one of our books—maybe a mistake in the text or the code—we would be grateful if you would report this to us. By doing so, you can save other readers from frustration and help us improve subsequent versions of this book. If you find any errata, please report them by visiting `http://www.packtpub.com/submit-errata`, selecting your book, clicking on the **errata submission form** link, and entering the details of your errata. Once your errata are verified, your submission will be accepted and the errata will be uploaded on our website, or added to any list of existing errata, under the Errata section of that title. Any existing errata can be viewed by selecting your title from `http://www.packtpub.com/support`.

Piracy

Piracy of copyright material on the Internet is an ongoing problem across all media. At Packt, we take the protection of our copyright and licenses very seriously. If you come across any illegal copies of our works, in any form, on the Internet, please provide us with the location address or website name immediately so that we can pursue a remedy.

Please contact us at `copyright@packtpub.com` with a link to the suspected pirated material.

We appreciate your help in protecting our authors, and our ability to bring you valuable content.

Questions

You can contact us at `questions@packtpub.com` if you are having a problem with any aspect of the book, and we will do our best to address it.

1
Data Structure

This book will take you step-by-step through the process of building a clear and user-friendly sales management database in Ext JS using information from an existing database.

This book is intended for intermediate Ext JS developers with operational knowledge of MySQL and who want to improve their programming skills and create a higher-level application.

The finished application will give you a working sales management database. However, the true value of this book is the hands-on process of creating the application, and the opportunity to easily transfer and incorporate features introduced in this book in your own future applications.

The standout features we will look at while building this application are as follows:

- **History-supported back button functionality**: We will customize the Ext JS function to create a lighter method to scroll forwards and backwards while staying on a single page.

- **More efficient screen management**: We'll learn how simply registering a screen and naming conventions can help you cut down on the screen change processes; meaning you can focus more on the implementation behind each screen. Also, it will be easier to interact with the history just by conforming to this architecture.

- **Communication methods with Ext.Direct**: Ext.Direct has a close affinity with Ext applications which makes for easier connection, easier maintenance, and removes the need for the client side to change the URL. Also, if you use Ext.Direct, you can reduce the stress on the server side as it combines multiple server requests into just one request.

- **Data display methods with charts**: In Ext JS, by simply adjusting the store and the data structure set to display in a grid, we can display the data graphically in a chart.

This chapter will give you the basic building blocks of your database. In this chapter of the book, you will write the SQL code and and create tables in MySQL.

The structure of the application – User, Customer, Quotation, Quotations, Bill, and Bills

First, let's look at the structure of the application we're about to build. This is a sales management application built for the user to register customers, send quotations for orders, and finally to invoice the customer with a bill.

The user can input data in to the Customer table. The customer can be an individual or a company, either way, each customer receives a unique ID.

The Quotation table represents the final quotation sent to the customer. The Quotations table contains the individual items being ordered in the quotation.

A bill is the final invoice sent to the customer. As with the Quotations table, the Bills table refers to the individual items ordered by the customer.

The user

The user data is a simple structure that is used to log in to a system. It has an e-mail address, a password, and a name.

Do not delete the user data and physically manage it with a flag. It is connected to other data structures with joint ownership, recording the date and time when it was created along with the updated date and time.

When we design a table with a model of MySQL, it looks similar to the following table. After having carried out MD5, we perform SHA1. Then, we will have 40 characters and can store the password.

Name	Type	Length	Allow Null	Key
id	bigint	20		YES
status	tinyint	1		
email	varchar	255		
password	char	40		
lastname	varchar	20		
firstname	varchar	20		
modified	datetime	0	YES	
created	datetime	0		

The customer

The customer data contains the name and address of the company or client. It lets the Quotation and Bill tables perform a relation of this data and use the data. Being the master data, adding to and deleting from the user interface is not available at this time. However, as you develop the application, you eventually should be able to edit this data.

The following screenshot shows the input fields for registering a customer. The sections under the Name column are the fields that need to be filled in for each customer. The Type column refers to the type of data to be entered, such as words, numbers, and dates. The Key column allows data to be referenced between different tables.

Name	Type	Length	Allow Null	Key
id	bigint	20		YES
status	tinyint	1		
name	varchar	255		
addr1	char	255		
addr2	varchar	255	YES	
city	varchar	50		
state	varchar	50		
zip	varchar	10		
country	varchar	50		
phone	varchar	50		
fax	varchar	50	YES	
modified	datetime	0	YES	
created	datetime	0		

Quotation and Quotations

The Quotation and Quotations tables have a 1-N relationship.

In Quotation, you can save the basic information of the document, and in Quotations you can store each item being ordered.

Quotation

This following screenshot shows the fields necessary for `Quotation`. The table headings are the same as in the `Customer` table explained previously, so let's fill this out accordingly.

Name	Type	Length	Allow Null	Key
id	bigint	20		YES
status	tinyint	1		
company	bigint	20		
note	text	0		
modified	datetime	0	YES	
created	datetime	0		

Quotations

This is the same as before, so let's go ahead and fill this out. The parent refers to the overall quotation that the `Quotations` (individual items) table belongs to.

Name	Type	Length	Allow Null	Key
id	bigint	20		YES
status	tinyint	1		
parent	bigint	20		
description	varchar	255		
qty	int	11		
price	int	11		
sum	int	11		
modified	datetime	0	YES	
created	datetime	0		

Bill and Bills

The `Bill` table is almost the same as the `Quotation` table. However, the `Bill` table can sometimes contain the ID of an associated `Quotation` table.

Bill

The following screenshot shows the `Bill` table:

Name	Type	Length	Allow Null	Key
id	bigint	20		YES
status	tinyint	1		
quotation	bigint	20	YES	
company	char	20		
note	text	0		
modified	datetime	0	YES	
created	datetime	0		

Bills

Similar to `Quotations`, in `Bills` you can store each item that is ordered:

Name	Type	Length	Allow Null	Key
id	bigint	20		YES
status	tinyint	1		
parent	bigint	20		
description	varchar	255		
qty	int	11		
price	int	11		
sum	int	11		
modified	datetime	0	YES	
created	datetime	0		

Creating and dealing with the customer structure tables

We will be using MySQL, and the database character is set to utf8 and collation is set to utf8_bin. When SQL describes the details of what we defined previously, each of these components are as follows.

The User table

The User table we prepared earlier becomes operational when the following code is executed. It's important to remember to include AUTO_INCREMENT in the id column; otherwise, you have to input it manually:

```
SET NAMES utf8;
SET FOREIGN_KEY_CHECKS = 0;

DROP TABLE IF EXISTS 'users';
CREATE TABLE 'users' (
  'id' bigint(20) NOT NULL AUTO_INCREMENT,
  'status' tinyint(1) NOT NULL DEFAULT '1',
  'email' varchar(255) NOT NULL,
  'passwd' char(40) NOT NULL,
  'lastname' varchar(20) NOT NULL,
  'firstname' varchar(20) NOT NULL,
  'modified' datetime DEFAULT NULL,
  'created' datetime NOT NULL,
  PRIMARY KEY ('id')
) ENGINE=InnoDB DEFAULT CHARSET=utf8 ROW_FORMAT=DYNAMIC;

SET FOREIGN_KEY_CHECKS = 1;
```

The Customer table

Once the following code is executed, the Customer table becomes operational:

```
SET NAMES utf8;
SET FOREIGN_KEY_CHECKS = 0;

DROP TABLE IF EXISTS 'customers';
CREATE TABLE 'customers' (
  'id' bigint(20) NOT NULL AUTO_INCREMENT,
  'status' tinyint(1) NOT NULL DEFAULT '1',
  'name' varchar(255) NOT NULL,
  'addr1' varchar(255) NOT NULL,
  'addr2' varchar(255) DEFAULT NULL,
  'city' varchar(50) NOT NULL,
```

```
    'state' varchar(50) NOT NULL,
    'zip' varchar(10) NOT NULL,
    'country' varchar(50) NOT NULL,
    'phone' varchar(50) NOT NULL,
    'fax' varchar(50) DEFAULT NULL,
    'modified' datetime DEFAULT NULL,
    'created' datetime NOT NULL,
    PRIMARY KEY ('id')
) ENGINE=InnoDB DEFAULT CHARSET=utf8 ROW_FORMAT=DYNAMIC;

SET FOREIGN_KEY_CHECKS = 1;
```

This is the foundation of creating an initial set of tables that can later be populated with data.

The Quotation table

This is the corresponding code for the Quotation table. As with the Customer table, this code snippet will lay the foundation of our table.

```
SET NAMES utf8;
SET FOREIGN_KEY_CHECKS = 0;

DROP TABLE IF EXISTS 'quotation';
CREATE TABLE 'quotation' (
    'id' bigint(20) NOT NULL AUTO_INCREMENT,
    'status' tinyint(1) NOT NULL DEFAULT '1',
    'customer' bigint(20) NOT NULL,
    'note' text NOT NULL,
    'modified' datetime DEFAULT NULL,
    'created' datetime NOT NULL,
    PRIMARY KEY ('id')
) ENGINE=InnoDB DEFAULT CHARSET=utf8 ROW_FORMAT=DYNAMIC;

DROP TABLE IF EXISTS 'quotations';
CREATE TABLE 'quotations' (
    'id' bigint(20) NOT NULL AUTO_INCREMENT,
    'status' tinyint(1) NOT NULL DEFAULT '1',
    'parent' bigint(20) NOT NULL,
    'description' varchar(255) NOT NULL,
    'qty' int(11) NOT NULL,
    'price' int(11) NOT NULL,
    'sum' int(11) NOT NULL,
    'modified' datetime DEFAULT NULL,
    'created' datetime NOT NULL,
```

```
    PRIMARY KEY ('id'),
    KEY 'parent' ('parent')
) ENGINE=InnoDB DEFAULT CHARSET=utf8 ROW_FORMAT=DYNAMIC;

SET FOREIGN_KEY_CHECKS = 1;
```

The Bill table

As with the previous two code snippets, the following code for the `Bill` table is very similar to the `Quotation` table, so this can be found in the source file under `04_bill_table.sql`.

These are all the tables we need for this database. Now let's move on to testing after creating each operation.

Creating each operation and testing

Because we will use PHP in later stages, let's prepare each operation now. Here, we will insert some temporary data.

Remember to check that the acquisition and update operations are working properly.

User authentication

These are some SQL code you can use to develop your database.

You can look for a user by inputting an e-mail address and password. You can assume it was successful if the count is 1.

For increased password security, after having carried out MD5 encryption, you should store the password as a character string of 40 characters after being put through SHA1.

```
SELECT
    COUNT(id) as auth
FROM
    users
WHERE
    users.email = 'extkazuhiro@xenophy.com'
AND
    users.passwd = SHA1(MD5('password'))
AND
    users.status = 1;
```

Selecting the user list

This is used when you want to collect data for use in a grid. Make note of the fact that we are not performing the limit operation with `PagingToolbar`:

```
SELECT
    users.id,
    users.email,
    users.lastname,
    users.firstname
FROM
    users
WHERE
    users.status = 1;
```

Adding users

To add a user, put the current time in `created` and `modified`:

```
INSERT INTO users (
    email,
    passwd,
    lastname,
    firstname,
    modified,
    created
) VALUES (
    'someone@xenophy.com',
    SHA1(MD5('password')),
    'Kotsutsumi',
    'Kazuhiro',
    NOW(),
    NOW()
);
```

Updating the user information

Every time the `modified` file should be set to `NOW()` for it to be used as a time stamp. Other fields should be updated as needed.

```
UPDATE
    users
SET
    email='extkazuhiro@xenophy.com',
    passwd=SHA1(MD5('password')),
    lastname='Kotsutsumi',
```

```
    firstname='Kazuhiro',
    modified=NOW()
WHERE
    id=1
```

Deleting users

Deletion from this system is not a hard purge where the user data is permanently deleted. Instead we will use a soft purge, where the user data is not displayed after deletion but remains in the system. Therefore, note that we will use UPDATE, not DELETE. In the following code, status=9 denotes that the user has been deleted but not displayed. (status=1 will denote that the user is active).

```
UPDATE
    users
SET
    status=9
WHERE
    id=1
```

The Customers table

Although Add, Update, and Delete are necessary operations, we'll come to these in the later chapter, so we can leave it out at this time.

The customer information list

Here we are preparing the SQL code to pull information about customers later on:

```
SELECT
    customers.id,
    customers.name,
    customers.addr1,
    customers.addr2,
    customers.city,
    customers.state,
    customers.zip,
    customers.country,
    customers.phone,
    customers.fax
FROM
    customers
WHERE
    customers.status = 1;
```

Selecting the quotation list

Next comes the code for selecting the Quotation lists. This is similar to what we saw for the customer information list. For the code, please refer to the source file under `11_selecting_quotation_list.sql`.

Items

The code for items will select the quotation items from the database. This will pick up items where quotations.status is 1 and quotation.parent is 1:

```
SELECT quotations.description,
   quotations.qty,
   quotations.price,
   quotations.sum
FROM
   quotations
WHERE
   quotations.'status' = 1
AND
   quotations.parent = 1
```

As this is similar to Customers, you can again leave out Add, Update, and Delete for now.

The Bill table

Again let's leave out Add, Update and Delete for now because the Bill table is similar to what preceded this.

It's straightforward to say that once a quotation has been accepted, a bill is produced. Therefore, in data structures such as ours, Quotation and Bill are related. The only difference is that Bill contains the extra Quotation ID to create the relationship between the two.

Also, remember the customer information list is almost the same as the quotation list.

Summary

In this chapter, we have defined the structure of the database we will use in this book.

You might have your own databases that you want to present in Ext JS. This is just a sample database that we can build on in the coming chapters.

In the next chapter we will begin the process of building the whole application. Don't worry, we'll explain each step.

Planning Application Design

2

In this chapter, we will set up the development environment of the project while introducing Sencha Cmd.

In this chapter, you will learn to:

- Design a simple application
- Optimize Ajax requests to use Ext Direct and `Ext.util.History` to control the screen with URL

Setting up Sencha Cmd and a local development environment

By setting up the local development environment with Sencha Cmd, when finally deploying the application, Sencha Cmd will only pick up the components being used. This will therefore optimize the final application.

With Sencha Cmd, you can run a native package for Sencha Touch, including scaffolding and building themes. Let's begin generating your project using Sencha Cmd.

1. Install the latest JAVA Runtime Environment that is available on `http://www.oracle.com/technetwork/java/javase/downloads/index.html` or JRE.
2. Install Compass available at `http://compass-style.org/`.
3. Install Sencha Cmd available at `http://www.sencha.com/products/sencha-cmd/download`.
4. Download Ext JS SDK available at `http://www.sencha.com/products/extjs/download/`.
5. Extract Ext JS SDK and locate it in a local directory of your choice. For example, you can create a top-level directory called `ext`.

A directory structure will be created as shown in the following screenshot. This time, we will use Ext JS 4.2.2 GPL.

The example is in Mac OS X. After installation, Sencha Cmd is located in the following path, `~/bin/Sencha/Cmd/4.0.0.203/`.

For Windows, Sencha Cmd is located at the following path, `C:/Users/(your username)/bin`.

If the path is set correctly, you should be able to execute the following command under Sencha and the following list of options, categories, and commands should appear on your screen.

```
# sencha
Sencha Cmd v4.0.0.203
```

By using a combination of the following definitions within Sencha Cmd, we can use Sencha Cmd.

For example, to create a project, using the options and categories we can enter, `sencha -sdk [/sdk/path] generate app App [/project/path]`.

To build a project, we can use categories and commands to enter: `sencha app build`.

Options

Here are some options you can use:

- * `--debug, -d -` : This sets the log level to higher verbosity
- * `--plain, -p -` : This enables plain logging output (no highlighting)
- * `--quiet, -q -` : This sets the log level to warnings and errors only
- * `--sdk-path, -s -` : This sets the path to the target framework

Categories

Here are some categories you can use:

- `*app -` : Using this, we can performs various application build processes
- `*compile -` : This allows us to compile sources to produce concatenated output and metadata
- `*fs -` : This is a set of useful utility actions to work with files
- `*generate -` : This generates models, controllers, and so on, or an entire application
- `*manifest -` : This extracts class metadata

- *package - : This packages a Sencha Touch application for native app stores

- *theme - : This builds a set of theme images from a given html page

Commands

Here are some commands you can use:

- * ant - : This invokes Ant with helpful properties back to Sencha Command

- * build - : This builds a project from a JSB3 file.

- * config - : This loads a config file or sets a configuration property

- * help - : This displays help for commands

- * js - : This executes arbitrary JavaScript file(s)

- * which - : This displays the path to the current version of Sencha Cmd

Creating a project with Sencha Cmd

To begin with, let's generate a project using Sencha Cmd. At first, move the current directory into the project directory and execute the following command:

```
# sencha -sdk ./ext generate app MyApp ./
```

The following log should present itself. It's very long, so this is an abridged version, that is, the start and the end of the log:

```
[INF]    init-properties:
[INF]    init-sencha-command:
[INF]    init:
.
.
.
[INF]    app-refresh:
[INF]    -after-generate-app:
[INF]    generate-app:
```

Then, a directory is generated as follows:

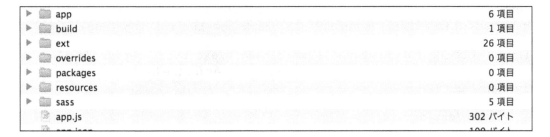

Let's look at it with a browser; it should be displayed as follows. By all means display it via a web server.

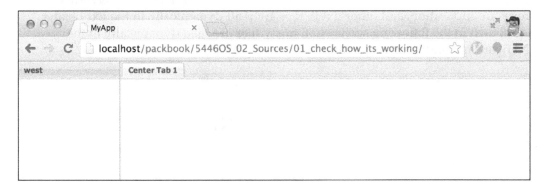

By executing the command, Sencha Cmd creates a temporary view and controller to get the whole project up and running quickly. We can make changes or additions to this to suit our own applications.

Creating a component test

The temporary application was generated in Sencha Cmd. However, you should not customize this immediately. Before you do, let's make a **component test** (CT) to facilitate development. Generally speaking, it tests the source code and the relationships between the components. The CT shows the source code being tested in the viewport and in separate test views, without moving the whole source code. By using a CT, a team of developers can smoothly build an application at the same time and detect problems early in the development process.

Check how it's working

First, you can check how the automatically generated application works and look at the details of `index.html` (source file: `01_check_how_its_working/index.html`).

The only CSS file that can be read is `ext/packages/ext-theme-neptune/build/resources/ext-theme-neptune-all-debug.css`. As for the JS file, the following three are read.

- `ext/ext-dev.js`
- `bootstrap.js`
- `app/app.js`

To run `app.js`, you need `ext-dev.js` and `bootstrap.js`. These are necessary for your application, and other Ext JS files are read dynamically in the Ext Loader. As shown in the following screenshot, many files are read dynamically in the **Network** tab under developer tools in the Google Chrome browser:

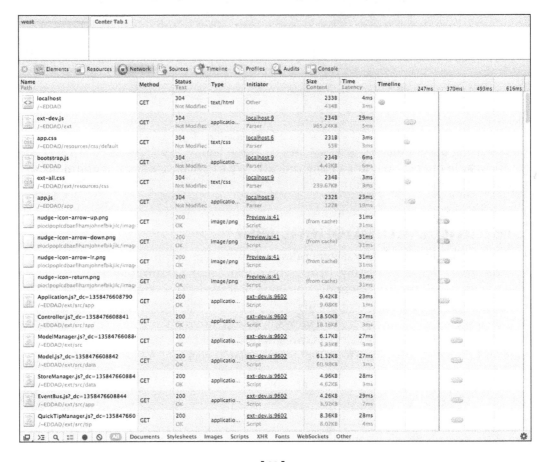

This time we will use the Ext JS Neptune theme to build the application.

When you make a new application, the default theme `ext-theme-classic` is used. Let's change that to `ext-theme-neptune`.

The target file to modify is as follows:

`.sencha/app/sencha.cfg - L32`

```
# The name of the package containing the theme scss for the app
app.theme=ext-theme-classic
```

Change the previous line to the following:

```
# The name of the package containing the theme scss for the app
app.theme=ext-theme-neptune
```

When you proceed to the next section after making this change, the theme should be changed. The theme will look like the following screenshot:

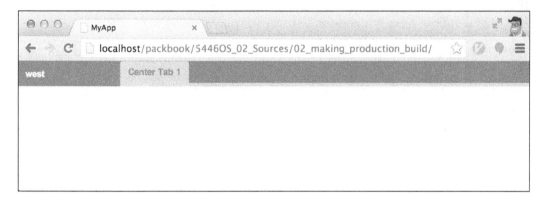

Making production build

When you use Ext Loader, it takes a lot of time before a screen is displayed. It becomes slower as the scale of the application grows and the number of files increases. This might be too slow for the product.

But have no fear, you already have the solution at hand — build with Sencha Cmd. First, move the current project into the project directory and execute the following command:

```
# sencha app build
```

The following directory is made when you execute the command:

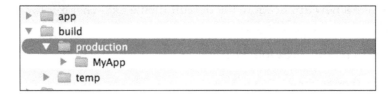

The `app.js` file generated here is a minified JavaScript file that combines the code that you write with the Ext JS SDK. Enabling `app.js` is effective because the code has already been read and the Ext Loader does not need to read the code again, improving speed. This `app.js` file is generated in a compressed state that removes unnecessary new lines.

The `./build/production/MyApp/` directory was generated and stored. Let's check the generated production application with a browser.

If you want to debug, it's a very bad idea to compress `app.js`. Instead, you should execute the following command for testing:

```
# sencha app build testing
```

The `testing` directory is then made in the same directory as `production` as shown in the following screenshot. The `app.js` file made under this directory is not compressed.

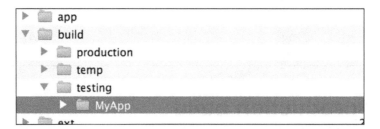

CT in individual views

If you conduct a CT in the normal way, you will have to test all the components at the same time. However, if we split the CT into individual views, we can test each component individually in its own HTML.

First, we create a directory called `ct` and write HTML for the components lists. It is simply the `index.html` code in the source file: `03_ct_in_individual_views/ct/index.html`.

Here, you will make a header component. First let's create its appearance. You can make a ct directory for the header components as in the following screenshot:

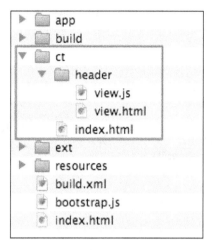

Create view.html and view.js in the header file. The code is given as follows:

```
view.html
<html>
<head>
<meta charset="utf-8" />
<title>[View]Header - Component Test</title>
<link rel="stylesheet" href="../../bootstrap.css" type="text/css">
<script language="JavaScript" type="text/javascript" src="../../ext/
ext-all.js"></script>
</head>
<body>
<script type="text/javascript" src="./view.js"></script>
</body>
</html>
```

```
view.js
Ext.Loader.setConfig({
    enabled: true,
    paths: {
        MyApp: '../../app/'
    }
});

Ext.onReady(function() {
    Ext.create('MyApp.view.Header', {
        renderTo: Ext.getBody()
    });
});
```

View component

Let's make the header component `MyApp.view.Header`. You should make the `Header.js` under the `app/view` directory and create the `Header` component (source file: `04_view_component/app/view/Header.js`).

```
Ext.define('MyApp.view.Header', {
    extend: 'MyApp.toolbar.Toolbar',
    alias: 'widget.myapp-header',
    height: 35,
    items: [{
        text: 'MyApp',
        action: 'dashboard'
    }, '->', {
        text: 'MyAccount',
        action: 'myaccount'
    }, {
        text: 'Log Out',
        action: 'logout'
    }]
});
```

When you create the `MyApp.toolbar.Toolbar` class, the panel component in `MyApp` will work. Therefore, make a panel directory under the `app` directory (source file: `04_view_component/app/toolbar/Toolbar.js`).

```
Ext.define('MyApp.toolbar.Toolbar', {
    extend: 'Ext.toolbar.Toolbar'
});
```

When you display it with a browser, the following screenshot will appear:

At this point, even if you click on the buttons, nothing will happen because you still need to implement the event handler; but don't worry, we'll get to that.

Adding controllers

The appearance has been made. So now, let's add a controller. To do this, make `Abstract.js` under the `app/controller` directory, followed by the `MyApp.controller.Abstract` class (source file: `05_adding_controller/app/controller/Abstract.js`).

```
Ext.define('MyApp.controller.Abstract', {
    extend: 'Ext.app.Controller'
});
```

Adding controllers is very simple, it merely extends to `Ext.app.Controller`. This class will implement all the common features for the controllers, which we will create from now on. So, let's make a controller for the header. Make `Header.js` in the same directory and define it as `MyApp.controller.Header`. In the following code, from the `MyApp.controller.Abstract` class, which we made some time ago, the `init` method is implemented (source file: `05_adding_controller/app/controller/Header.js`).

```
Ext.define('MyApp.controller.Header', {
    extend: 'MyApp.controller.Abstract',
    init: function() {
        var me = this;
        me.control({
            'myapp-header [action=dashboard]': {
                click: function() {
                    console.log('dashboard');
                }
            },
            'myapp-header [action=myaccount]': {
                click: function () {
                    console.log('myaccount');
                }
            },
            'myapp-header [action=logout]': {
                click: function() {
                    console.log('logout');
                }
            }
        });
    }
});
```

The following are the component queries from the previous code. These acquire buttons located in header. With this, you have now finished making the controller.

```
'myapp-header [action=dashboard]'
'myapp-header [action=myaccount]'
'myapp-header [action=logout]'
```

A file should be created as shown in the following screenshot:

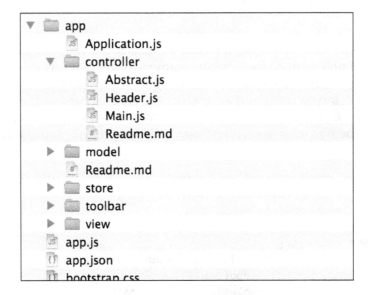

Let's make the CT operate the controller that you made successfully. In the directory, where you created `view.html` and `view.js`, you should now create `app.html` and `app.js`. The `app.html` CT is mostly the same as for `view.html`. You can see the source code here: `06_app_test/ct/header/app.html`.

For `app.js`, please see the following code (source file: `06_app_test/ct/header/app.js`).

```
Ext.application({
    autoCreateViewport: false,
    name: 'MyApp',
    appFolder: '../../app',
    controllers: [
        'Header'
    ],
    launch: function() {
        var panel = Ext.create('MyApp.view.Header', {
            renderTo: Ext.getBody()
```

```
        });
        Ext.util.Observable.capture(panel, function() {
            console.log(arguments);
        });
    }
});
```

You should add a link for `app.html` to `index.html` in the `ct` directory. In `app.js`, call `Ext.application` and start the application only for headers. Because the `autoCreateViewport` default value is set to `true`, you should set it to `false`. This is because `Viewport` is unnecessary for this test.

Second, set header to read `MyApp.controller.Header` in controllers. You should set the function to launch to create a view. The `Ext.util.Observable.capture` call captures the event that is fired in an object set in the first argument.

We can confirm visually that an event reacts when you click on the buttons.

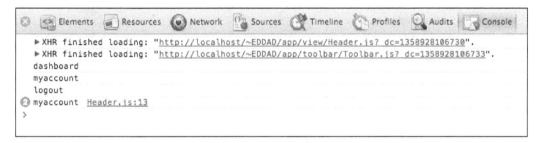

We just made a view without a controller. The reason is if we create a relationship between the controller and the view at this stage, it would make it very difficult to test the view.

We made `app.html` that includes the controller logic. We need the `app.html` to be able to test the view and the controller at the same time.

In addition, to avoid incorrect code referring to a direct object, divide each component and each screen that you can put together in the CT and develop it in the viewport later.

Now, let's learn to create a component and a CT in sequence.

Creating views

We need to create the appearance of the application. You already made the header. Let's put the navigation menu for the application on the left of the screen. Locate the header you made previously on the top of the screen. Name the screen that is in the center region but to the right. Put the screen in this center region.

The screen is divided into four sections:

- Dashboard
- MyAccount
- Quotation
- Bill

Connect these four and make a rough view structure as shown in the following diagram:

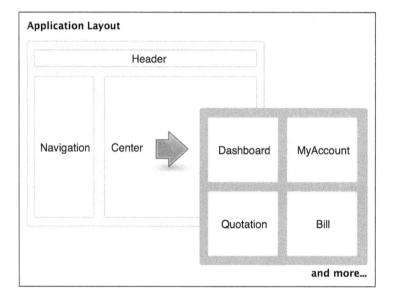

Navigation

Let's make the navigation section. This component extends a tree panel. By using a tree panel, the procedure to display the menu options can be handled by the server, rather than inputting menu options manually. The process of dividing the menu options into groups can be made simpler.

A tree store is necessary for a tree panel. So let's make it now (source file: `07_creating_views/app/store/Navigation.js`).

```
Ext.define('MyApp.store.Navigation', {
    extend: 'Ext.data.TreeStore',
    storeId: 'Navigation',
    root: {
        expanded: true,
        children: [{
            text: 'Dashboard',
            leaf: true
        }, {
            text: 'Quotation',
            leaf: true
        }, {
            text: 'Bill',
            leaf: true
        }, {
            text: 'MyAccount',
            leaf: true
        }]
    }
});
```

Now that a store has been made, you can define the tree panel (source file: `07_creating_views/app/view/Navigation.js`).

```
Ext.define('MyApp.view.Navigation', {
    extend: 'Ext.tree.Panel',
    alias: 'widget.myapp-navigation',
    title: 'Navigation',
    store: 'Navigation',
    rootVisible: false,
    animate: false
});
```

Now, let's create a CT to check what we made. The code for `07_creating_views/ct/navigation/view.html` is very similar to the previous `view.html` code, so please refer to the source file if you want to see this. The following code is for `view.js` (source file: `07_creating_views/ct/navigation/view.js`):

```
Ext.onReady(function() {
    Ext.create('MyApp.store.Navigation', {
        storeId: 'Navigation'
    });
    Ext.create('MyApp.view.Navigation', {

    });
});
```

We previously created a store because it is necessary to display the navigation view. The **Navigation** view is displayed like in the following screenshot when we see it in a browser:

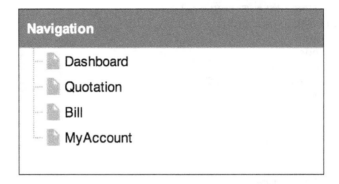

Let's make the remaining components in the same way as follows.

Dashboard

We want to make a panel for dashboards (we will make many similar panels from now on). Therefore, the application will be made in the MyApp.panel.Screen abstract class. The MyApp.panel.Screen abstract class is the fundamental mold for the whole application (source file: 07_creating_views/app/panel/Screen.js).

```
Ext.define('MyApp.panel.Screen', {
    extend: 'Ext.panel.Panel',
    initComponent: function() {
        var me = this;
        me.callParent(arguments);
    }
});
```

We were able to create the abstract class. Now, let's create a dashboard class that inherits from this abstract class (source file: 07_creating_views/app/view/DashBoard.js).

```
Ext.define('MyApp.view.DashBoard', {
    extend: 'MyApp.panel.Screen',
    alias: 'widget.myapp-dashboard'
});
```

Now, prepare the CT to check the appearance. Both 07_creating_views/ct/dashboard/view.html and 07_creating_views/ct/dashboard/view.js are similar to ct/header, so please refer to the source files for the code.

MyAccount

Let's make the user's personal account page. Let's call this "MyAccount" and create it in the same way as we created the dashboard. Apart from the alias property and the title property, it's exactly the same as the dashboard. For the code, please see the source file: `07_creating_views/app/view/MyAccount.js`.

Quotation and bill

Continue to make the quotation and bill in the same way. Again, besides the alias property and the title property, it's the same as the dashboard. Please see the source files for the code:

* `07_creating_views/app/view/Quotation.js`
* `07_creating_views/app/view/Bill.js`

Viewport

Let's compose the component that we made so far in the viewport. Revise the file, which was already generated automatically by Sencha Cmd. Although we can make a CT by all means, with the viewport, the CT is unnecessary. HTML in itself is the same as the CT index.

First, it is necessary to revise `app/Application.js` to use the navigation store (source file: `08_create_viewport/app/Application.js`).

```
Ext.define('MyApp.Application', {

    stores: [
        'Navigation'
    ]
});
```

For the `xtype` classes that are set in the viewport, it is necessary for the reading of the source code to have been completed in advance. So we have added the class names to the `application.js` file.

To reflect the CSS of the newly added component, we'll build the application once with Sencha Cmd. This will make sure that the CSS of any new components are included in `sencha app build`.

With this, the component style that is being allotted to the `bootstrap.css` will be renewed. It is displayed as shown in the following screenshot when we access `index.html`, which is under a document route. The files that we made are read dynamically in the Ext Loader.

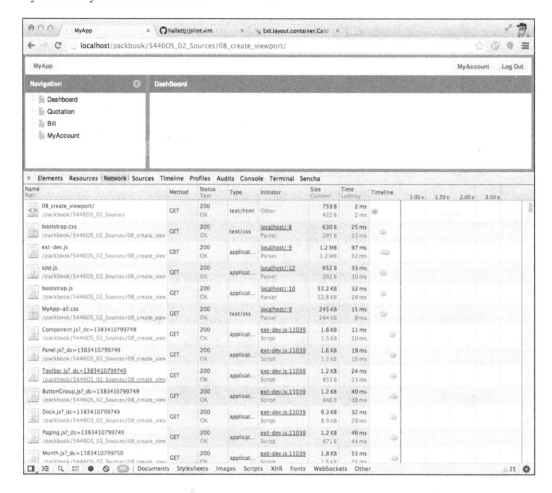

Now the views are complete!

Creating controllers

Now, we will create controllers for our data.

Main

Usually, each view component has a corresponding controller class with the same prefix.

But the first controller we have to deal with is the controller called Main. This controller has already been produced automatically in Sencha Cmd. If we need more processing or logic for the whole application, we should implement this class. Usually, the `view` class and controller class names match, but this is a special case where they do not because Sencha Cmd generates the Main class. So, it is best to leave it as is and not change the name.

For the `app/controller/Main.js` code, please see the source file: `09_create_controller\app\controller`.

Although we've talked a lot about Main, we are not going to use it for the time being.

Navigation

Now, let's add `hrefTarget` to the data in the navigation store (source file: `09_create_controller/app/store/Navigation.js`).

```
Ext.define('MyApp.store.Navigation', {
    ...
    root: {
        children: [{
            text: 'Dashboard',
            hrefTarget: '#!/dashboard',
            leaf: true
        }, {
            text: 'Quotation',
            hrefTarget: '#!/quotation',
            leaf: true
        }, {
            text: 'Bill',
            hrefTarget: '#!/bill',
            leaf: true
        }, {
            text: 'MyAccount',
            hrefTarget: '#!/myaccount',
            leaf: true
        }]
    }
});
```

Now, make a navigation controller and describe the `itemclick` event handler and catch an event when a menu is chosen (source file: `09_create_controller/app/controller/Navigation.js`).

```
Ext.define('MyApp.controller.Navigation', {
    extend: 'MyApp.controller.Abstract',
    init: function() {
        var me = this;
        me.control({
            'myapp-navigation': {
                itemclick: function(row, model) {
                    if (!model.isLeaf()) {
                        if (model.isExpanded()) {
                            model.collapse();
                        } else {
                            model.expand();
                        }
                    } else {
                        if (model.data.hrefTarget) {
                            console.log('select:' + model.data.
                            hrefTarget);
                        }
                    }
                }
            }
        });
    }
});
```

Add this to `app/Application.js` so that it is used when we display it in the viewport.

```
Ext.define('MyApp.Application', {

    controllers: [
        'Main',
        'Header',
        'Navigation',
        'DashBoard',
        'MyAccount',
        'Quotation',
        'Bill'
    ],

});
```

Furthermore, remember that the CT prepares to operate from the controller on its own. The following code will execute the CT for navigation (source code: `09_create_controller/ct/navigation/app.js`).

```
Ext.application({
    ...
    stores: [
        'Navigation'
    ],
    controllers: [
        'Navigation'
    ],
    launch: function() {
        var panel = Ext.create('MyApp.view.Navigation', {
            width: 300,
            height: 600,
            renderTo: Ext.getBody()
        });
        Ext.util.Observable.capture(panel, function() {
            console.log(arguments);
        });
    }
});
```

When we perform this, a message is displayed by the console when we select any option from the menu.

Dashboard

Let's continue now and create the controller for dashboard. We do not describe any special process here, it is just preparation. Just implement the following code (source file: `09_create_controller/app/controller/DashBoard.js`):

```
Ext.define('MyApp.controller.DashBoard', {
    extend: 'MyApp.controller.Abstract',
    init: function() {
        var me = this;
        me.control({
        });
    }
});
```

MyAccount

MyAccount is the same as dashboard, just replace `Dashboard` with `MyAccount`.
For the code, please see the source file: `09_create_controller/app/controller/`
`MyAccount.js`.

Quotation and bill

It's the same for the quotation and bill. No special processing, just preparation,
whichare also the same as the dashboard. For the code, please see the source file
at the following locations:

- `09_create_controller/app/controller/Quotation.js`

- `09_create_controller/app/controller/Bill.js`

At this point, you have made many files. As we created them, they filled the
directory as shown in the following screenshot:

Using Ext.util.History for directly accessing a screen

Ext.util.History manages the history. When a page changes, the application catches this change and then the Ext.util.History fires an event. Using this feature, we can control actions in our application.. For example, by using Ext.util.History, every time the application is accessed the dashboard URL is displayed.

Sometimes, when the user inputs an incorrect hash in the URL, the application will have trouble finding the page. However, with Ext.util.History, it goes to screens specified by the developer. For example, when we implement Ext.util.History, the user can access the quotation page directly without abnormal screen behavior. With Ext.util.History, it also allows us to attach the URL to an e-mail to access documents directly.

To begin with, you need to make the MyApp.util.History class. You might think it is an abstract class when you set eyes on it, actually, it is different. MyApp.util.History is a class used to incorporate URL control in our application using Ext.util.History. Be careful to not make a mistake here or MyApp.util.History will not work. The Ext.util.History class is a singleton class and MyApp.util.History will make a singleton class too. First, let's make the MyApp.util.History class. It is very simple (source file: 10_util_history/app/util/History.js).

```
Ext.define('MyApp.util.History', {
    singleton: true,
    uses: ['Ext.util.History'],
    controllers: {},
    init: ... (implement)
    initNavigate: ... (implement)
    navigate: ... (implement)
    parseToken: ... (implement)
    push ... (implement)
    cleanUrl ... (implement)
    back: ... (implement)
    location: ... (implement)
});
```

Let's implement the methods by implementing the following list:

- `init`
- `initNavigate`
- `navigate`
- `parseToken`
- `push`
- `cleanUrl`
- `back`
- `location`

Please implement them as a method of the `MyApp.util.History` class (source file: `10_util_history/app/util/History.js`). The code for the implementation of this list is too long to include in this text, so please refer to the source file for the code.

When we use `MyApp.util.History`, we have to call the `init` method. I will describe the usage of the `init` method later. We do not need too much explanation about these methods, as this will take too long. The important thing to know is that these methods are important for browser navigation.

Adding logic to the controller

Add `MyApp.util.History` and a constructor to `MyApp.controller.Abstract` (source file: `11_adding_controller/app/controller/Abstract.js`).

```
Ext.define('MyApp.controller.Abstract', {
    extend: 'Ext.app.Controller',
    uses: ['MyApp.util.History'],
    aliasPrefix: 'myapp-',
    constructor: function() {
        var me = this,
            screenName = me.screenName;

        Ext.apply(me, {
            history: MyApp.util.History
        });
        if (screenName) {
            me.history.controllers[screenName] = me;
            me.baseUrl = '#!/' + screenName;
            me.aliasName = me.aliasPrefix + screenName;
        }
        me.callParent(arguments);
    },
    loadIndex: function(url) {
```

```
            var me = this, url = url || me.baseUrl;
            if (url.substr(0, 2) !== '#!') {
                url = me.baseUrl + '/' + url;
            }
            me.history.push(url, {
                navigate: true,
                callback: function() {
                    var self = Ext.ComponentQuery.query(me.aliasName)[0];
                    self.fireEvent('myapp-show', self);
                }
            });
        },
        init: function() {
            var me = this, o = {};
            o[me.aliasName] = {
                'myapp-show': me.onShow,
                'myapp-hide': me.onHide
            };
            me.control(o);
        },
        onShow: function() {
            // Nothing todo
        },
        onHide: function() {
            // Nothing todo
        }
    });
```

Set an anonymity function called `MyApp.util.History.init`, which we made previously, and initialize it to launch. Specify the screen to use with the sequence in an argument (source file: `11_adding_controller/app/Application.js`).

```
Ext.define('MyApp.Application', {

    stores: [
        'Navigation'
    ],

    screens: [
        'dashboard',
        'myaccount',
        'quotation',
        'bill'
    ],
    launch: function() {
        MyApp.util.History.init({
            screens: this.screens
        });
    }
});
```

Afterwards, add the `screenName` property to each class (source file: `11_adding_controller/app/controller/DashBoard.js`).

```
Ext.define('MyApp.controller.DashBoard', {
    extend: 'MyApp.controller.Abstract',
    screenName: 'dashboard',

});
```

In the same way as with the dashboard, we'll add a `screenName` property to MyAccount, Quotation, and Bill. Check the source file for the code:

- `11_adding_controller/app/controller/MyAccount.js`

- `11_adding_controller/app/controller/Quotation.js`

- `11_adding_controller/app/controller/Bill.js`

Fix the navigation controller. We should change the locale by removing the console and changing the call to the location method in `MyApp.util.History` (source file: `11_adding_controller/app/controller/Navigation.js`).

```
Ext.define('MyApp.controller.Navigation', {
    extend: 'MyApp.controller.Abstract',
    init: function() {
        var me = this;
        me.control({
            'myapp-navigation': {
                itemclick: function(row, model) {
                    ...
                    if (model.data.hrefTarget) {
                        console.log('select:' + model.data.
                        hrefTarget);
                        me.history.location(model.data.
                        hrefTarget);
                    }

});
```

Finally, if we make a distinction between each view, it becomes easier to acquire that view. So let's add `itemId` to each view. First, let's add it to the dashboard (source file: `11_adding_controller/app/view/DashBoard.js`).

```
Ext.define('MyApp.view.DashBoard', {
    ...
    itemId: 'screen-dashboard',
    title: 'DashBoard'
});
```

Again, let's add the `itemId` in the same way for MyAccount, Quotation, and Bill. Check the following source files for the code:

- `11_adding_controller/app/view/MyAccount.js`
- `11_adding_controller/app/view/Quotation.js`
- `11_adding_controller/app/view/Bill.js`

So to confirm, we should see the URL with the added hash when we click on the navigation menu after we have set it up with `init`.

- `#!/dashboard`
- `#!/quotation`
- `#!/bill`
- `#!/myaccount`

Setting up Ext Direct

This is the last in the long list of preparations. Most Sencha Ext JS applications communicate with a server and acquire data and transmit a message. In that case, it is very simple and easy to communicate with the `Ext.Ajax` class.

However, let's use Ext Direct this time. Ext Direct performs by wrapping Ajax communications, polling, and performing a **Remote Procedure Call (RPC)**.

RPC is the main feature of Ext Direct. However, I will not discuss it in detail here because of lack of space. If you wish to know the specifics, please visit the Sencha homepage at `http://www.sencha.com/products/extjs/extdirect`.

Ext Direct simplifies the communication with the server. As a result, JavaScript code decreases. Also, in addition to the reading and burden on browsers being reduced, communication is optimized automatically by a combined request function.

When we simultaneously perform Ajax communication with an initial value via Ext Direct in an interval of 10 milliseconds, we can combine the requests to the router into one communication. But for us, it is the same as us communicating each request separately.

> This is still not common knowledge among a lot of developers, especially those who do not know about the benefits of Ext Direct. It is a shame because this is such a convenient feature to have in your application.
>
> It does take a lot of preparation in the beginning. However, the development of future Sencha Ext JS will become simpler if we learn it here and keep it prepared and available, like a template.

Creating the Ext Direct router

First we need to make the router and implement it in PHP from here. In fact, the router is implemented in a sample. We only locate it and use it for it to start. To begin, copy the PHP from the sample page. You can find the sample page in your Ext SDK path followed by `/examples/direct/`. In other words. it's `(Ext SDK path)/examples/direct/`.

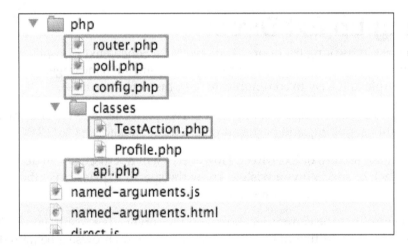

Create a folder called `php` in the document route and copy the four files shown in the previous screenshot. After we have copied the files, it is acceptable to delete them from this path.

Edit `config.php` and define the method as the class shown on the server side. There are so many interfaces in the original, but this time, we will use only one. So let's delete the others to keep things manageable (source file: `12_setup_ext_direct/php/config.php`).

```php
<?php
$API = array(
    'TestAction' => array(
        'methods' => array(
```

```
        'doEcho' => array(
            'len' => 1
        )
    )
)
);
```

Creating the Ext Direct module

In the same way as we did previously, we'll only use the doEcho method in the
TestAction class. So, let's delete the other methods to keep everything manageable
(source file: 12_setup_ext_direct/php/classes/TestAction.php).

```php
<?php
class TestAction {
    function doEcho($data) {
        return $data;
    }
}
```

Applying Ext Direct to the client application

Now, set the client application to immediately call TestAction.doEcho from
the client side by adding the following source code in index.html (source file:
12_setup_ext_direct/index.html).

```
    . . .
<!-- </x-compile> -->
<script src="php/api.php"></script>
</head>
```

Next, call addProvider and set it to use a member shown in the server side in
Application.js (source file: 12_setup_ext_direct/app/Application.js).

```js
Ext.require([
    'Ext.direct.*',
    'Ext.data.proxy.Direct',
    'Ext.form.action.DirectSubmit'
]);

Ext.onReady(function() {
    Ext.direct.Manager.addProvider(Ext.app.REMOTING_API);
});

Ext.define('MyApp.Application', {
```

Testing Ext Direct

Now we can test it. When a logout button is clicked, call `doEcho` and confirm whether it works normally. Then, add the processing to the header controller.

Check the performance with a browser. When we click on the logout button, the character string `message` already in the code will be sent to the server side. We can then check to see if `message` comes back to the client side. If it comes back successfully, everything is good! For reference, please check the source file: `12_setup_ext_direct/app/controller/Header.js`.

Summary

Good work! We are now ready to develop the application. It was very long, but remember, it only takes a long time to complete the initial preparations.

From now on, you can use what you did here in the future. If you go over what we have just done and understand it for yourself, you can use this as a template for future projects and it will make the preparation stage go a lot faster and smoother.

When you're ready, continue to the next chapter in which we'll begin to input data into our database.

3
Data Input

Welcome back. So, in the previous two chapters we worked on data structures and we made tables in SQL and MySQL. Then we created the development environment while getting to grips with Sencha Cmd.

In this chapter, we will:

- Learn to make a form to input data
- Transmit that data to a server via Ext Direct
- Learn about monitoring the state of the input
- Learn how to use Ext Direct to validate the `MyAccount` form on the server side

Creating the login page

Let's start by creating the login page for this application. Here we will perform a simple implementation using PHP. We will create `login.php` and `logout.php`. However, we will not go into too much detail about the login logic here because this book is focused on Ext JS and not PHP.

Create the variable you will input in SQL and then just pull the user information from the database.

The source code is very long, so please go to the source file to view the `login.php` file from the `01_making_the_login` folder and `logout.php` from `01_making_the_login`.

Store the user data for the session with the key USERINFO. Again, to be able to perform a login check, change index.html to index.php and run the login check. Apart from the PHP code at the beginning, it's the same as index.html (source file: 01_making_the_login/index.php):

```php
<?php
session_start();
if(!isset($_SESSION['USERINFO'])) {
    header("Location: ./login.php");
}
?>
<!DOCTYPE HTML>
...
</html>
```

Creating the MyAccount form

Now, let's build the forms that will deploy to various screens. First comes MyAccount.

Add the form panel to the temporary panel you built. Don't install the form directly onto the Screen panel — there is a reason to this. You will make relationships between the list and the details, so there are times when there are numerous panels existing inside the screen.

It just so happens that MyAccount only needs one screen. If the number of methods increases, there is a chance that you will need multiple panels. You might need a panel to run the input verification. But it's difficult to say for sure at this point. So, it is necessary to make the **screen layout** into a **card layout** which will make it easier to handle multiple screens.

First, let's specify the screen layout to be a card layout. In the MyAccount.js script at the bottom of the view directory you made before, create a MyAccount directory and move into it. The hierarchy of the directory will change, so let's modify the class name as well (source file: 02_making_the_account_form/app/view/myaccount/MyAccount.js):

```js
Ext.define('MyApp.view.myaccount.MyAccount', {
extend: 'MyApp.panel.Screen',
    ....
```

Let's modify the class name as follows (Source file: `02_making_the_account_form/ app/controller/myaccount/MyAccount.js`):

```
Ext.define('MyApp.controller.myaccount.MyAccount', {
    extend: 'MyApp.controller.Abstract',
    ....
```

In the same way, edit the controllers of `Quotation`, `Bill`, and `Dashboard` and views. By doing this, the application should now be working.

Because the package name has changed, let's modify the `Application.js` controller settings accordingly (source file: `02_making_the_account_form/app/ Application.js`):

```
Ext.application({
    ....
    controllers: [
        'Main',
        'Header',
        'Navigation',
        'dashboard.Dashboard',
        'myaccount.MyAccount',
        'quotation.Quotation',
        'bill.Bill'
    ],
    ....
```

Also, the view name has changed, so we have to modify that as well (source file: `02_making_the_account_form/app/view/Viewport.js`):

```
Ext.define('MyApp.view.Viewport', {
    ....
    requires:[
        'Ext.panel.Panel',
        'Ext.layout.container.Border',
        'MyApp.view.Header',
        'MyApp.view.Navigation',
        'MyApp.view.dashboard.Dashboard',
        'MyApp.view.myaccount.MyAccount',
        'MyApp.view.quotation.Quotation',
        'MyApp.view.bill.Bill'
    ],
    ....
```

Now with this, we're free to make the form. To begin with, we want to create the form panel and put it into MyAccount, but we want to perform a data abstraction of the form panel. So, at the beginning let's do just that and create a simple inheritance.

In the same way as we created the class for app/panel/Screen.js, we'll create a class that's inherited from Ext.form.Panel (refer to the source file: 02_making_the_account_form/app/form/Panel.js).

We have created the inheritance. Let's make the edit panel (source file: 02_making_the_account_form/app/view/myaccount/Edit.js):

```
Ext.define('MyApp.view.myaccount.MyAccount', {
    extend: 'MyApp.form.Panel',
    alias : 'widget.myapp-myaccount-edit',
    itemId: 'screen-myaccount-edit',
    initComponent: function() {
        var me = this;
        Ext.apply(me, {
        });
        me.callParent(arguments);
    }
});
```

Let's perform the implementation inside the form a little later. First, let's embed this panel (source file: 02_making_the_account_form/app/view/myaccount/MyAccount.js):

```
Ext.define('MyApp.view.myaccount.MyAccount', {
    ...
    requires: [
        'MyApp.view.myaccount.Edit'
    ],
    itemId: 'screen-myaccount',
    title: 'MyAccount',
    layout: 'card',
    items: [{
        xtype: 'myapp-myaccount-edit',
        border: false
    }]
});
```

Make sure that there are no errors coming from the browser. The appearance does not change, so it might not be so interesting presently.

At the moment, it looks good on the display, but you might have noticed that a **CT** error has arisen. This is because we changed the name earlier. Let's fix this now.

The `MyAccount` class (`view` and `controller`) package name has changed, so go ahead and amend the following class names (check the source file for reference):

`02_making_the_account_form/ct/myaccount/view.js`

`02_making_the_account_form/ct/myaccount/app.js`

Along with this, you should also fix the other CT error.

Now, let's start to build the main form. When you define the classes, you can define them using the configuration options, but let's set it up using `Ext.apply` inside `initComponent`. If we set up the configuration with `initComponent`, we can set a more flexible variety of behaviors to the component when we create it.

The following code is really similar to the code that comes out of **Sencha Architect** (source file: `02_making_the_account_form/app/view/myaccount/Edit.js`):

```
Ext.define('MyApp.view.myaccount.Edit', {
    ...
    initComponent: function() {
        var me = this;
        // Fields
        Ext.apply(me, {
            bodyPadding: 20,
            defaultType: 'textfield',
            items: [{
                fieldLabel: 'email'
            }, {
                fieldLabel: 'firstname'
            }, {
                fieldLabel: 'lastname'
            }]
        });
        // TopToolbar
    Ext.apply(me, {
        tbar: [{
    text: 'Save',
    action: 'save'
            }, {
            text: 'Reset',
            action: 'reset'
            }]
        });
    me.callParent(arguments);
    }
});
```

If you run the preceding code, it will look like the following screenshot:

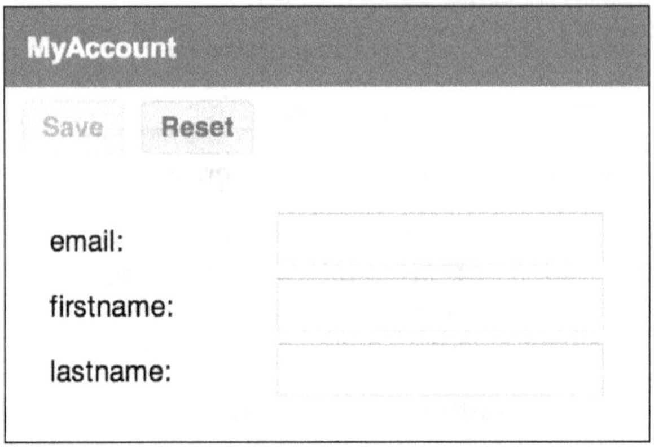

We make forms in this manner. Try adjusting it for yourself if you think up a more complex or attractive form. You can find more complex layouts published on *Sencha Ext samples*: http://dev.sencha.com/deploy/ext-4.0.0/examples/#sample-13.

At the moment, we see just three fields: **email:**, **firstname,** and **lastname:**. These are not usually modified often, but as we develop the application, other fields that require more modification might need to be added. In such occasions, you can add new fields in myaccount.Edit.

Creating the Quotation form

Let's continue and create forms for Quotation and Bill. In the same way as before, first set up the card layout in the Screen panel.

In the same way as with view/myaccount/MyAccount.js, in the Quotation class we will add the Edit and List screens (source file: 03_making_the_quotation_form/app/view/quotation/Quotation.js):

```
Ext.define('MyApp.view.quotation.Quotation', {
    ...
    requires: [
        'MyApp.view.quotation.List',
        'MyApp.view.quotation.Edit'
    ],
    ...
items: [{
        xtype: 'myapp-quotation-list',
        border: false
```

```
    }, {
            xtype: 'myapp-quotation-edit',
            border: false
    }]
});
```

Unlike the previous occasion, now two cards exist. These are `List` and `Edit`. You will implement `List` in a later chapter. Here, let's implement `Edit`.

The only thing is, if you don't create a class, then `requires` won't be able to read it. So, make a `List` class in the following way (source file: `03_making_the_quotation_ form/app/view/quotation/List.js`):

```
Ext.define('MyApp.view.quotation.List', {
    extend: 'MyApp.form.Panel',
    alias : 'widget.myapp-quotation-list',
    itemId: 'screen-quotation-list',
    initComponent: function() {
      var me = this;
      Ext.apply(me, {
        });
      me.callParent(arguments);
      }
});
```

Next, let's create `Edit`. It is a bit of a long process, so let's break it up into sections and go through each part (source file: `03_making_the_quotation_form/app/view/ quotation/Edit.js`):

```
Ext.define('MyApp.view.quotation.Edit', {
    extend: 'MyApp.form.Panel',
    alias : 'widget.myapp-quotation-edit',
    itemId: 'screen-quotation-edit',
    initComponent: function() {
      ...
      }
});
```

We have made an empty `MyApp.view.quotation.Edit` component and from now, we'll begin to implement the inside of the `initComponent` method. As we saw before, this will make the component more flexible.

Let's break this up into `Store`, `field` and `grid`, and `TopToolbar`. The following sections give the code that should be inserted into their specific points.

Store

The `Store` component is where the data will be stored locally in the browser.

Let's create the `Store` component now. Implement the following code into the `initComponent` method inside the `MyApp.view.quotation.Edit` class (source file: `03_making_the_quotation_form/app/view/quotation/Edit.js`):

```
Ext.applyIf(me, {
    customerStore: Ext.create('Ext.data.Store', {
        fields: ['id', 'name'],
        data : [
            {"id": 0, "name": "Sencha"},
            {"id": 1, "name": "Xenophy"}
        ]
    }),
    itemStore: Ext.create('Ext.data.Store', {
        storeId:'billItemStore',
        fields:['desc', 'qty', 'price', 'sum'],
        data:{'items':[
            { 'desc': 'Sencha Complete', "qty":"5", "price":"995",
              "sum": 4975 },
            { 'desc': 'Sencha Ext JS + Standard Support', "qty":"5",
              "price":"595", "sum": 2975 }
        ]},
proxy: {
type: 'memory',
reader: {
type: 'json',
root: 'items'
            }
        }
    })
});
```

Generate `customerStore` and `itemStore`. `customerStore` is made for the combobox and `itemStore` is made for the `grid` panel. Both stores are temporarily installed. That is why we're using `Ext.applyIf`. Let's modify this, so at a later stage you can acquire the data via Ext Direct.

The field and grid components

In this section, we will build the field components (in this case, it means the combobox along the top of the screen), and the grid panel that will appear below it.

It's a little bit long, but write the following after the previous step when we defined the Store component (source file: 03_making_the_quotation_form/app/view/quotation/Edit.js):

```
Ext.apply(me, {
    bodyPadding: 20,
    items: [{
        padding: '0 0 20 0',
        width: 500,
        xtype: 'combo',
        fieldLabel: 'customer',
        store: me.customerStore,
        editable: false,
        displayField: 'name',
        valueField: 'id'
    }, {
        // Grid Panel
        height: 400,
        padding: '0 0 20 0',
        xtype: 'grid',
        store: me.itemStore,
        plugins: [Ext.create('Ext.grid.plugin.CellEditing')],
        columns: [{
            text: 'Description',
            dataIndex: 'desc',
            flex: 1,
            editor: true
        }, {
            text: 'Qty',
            dataIndex: 'qty',
            editor: {
                xtype: 'numberfield',
                allowBlank: false,
                minValue: 0,
                maxValue: 10000
            }
        }, {
            text: 'Price',
            dataIndex: 'price',
```

```
            renderer: Ext.util.Format.usMoney,
            editor: {
                xtype: 'numberfield',
                allowBlank: false,
                minValue: 0,
                maxValue: 10000
            }
        }, {
            text: 'Sum',
            dataIndex: 'sum',
            renderer: Ext.util.Format.usMoney
        }],
        tbar: [{
            text: 'Add Item',
            action: 'add-item'
        }, '-', {
            text: 'Remove Item',
            action: 'remove-item'
        }]
    }, {
        fieldLabel: 'note',
        xtype: 'textarea',
        width: 500j
    }]
});
```

If you lay out the field, you are laying out the `grid` panel. The point to remember here is that the `grid` panel is set up with the plugin `Ext.grid.plugin.CellEditing`. In order to open various cells to edit, we have set up the editor key in the column settings. The `textfield` form field is used by default, but you want just numerical inputs in `qty` and `price`, so we are using `numberfield` for those.

TopToolbar

In this section we will create the `Save` button that will go on the top toolbar in our application.

To do this, write the following code after the code we wrote in the previous step to display the `Save` button (source file: `03_making_the_quotation_form/app/view/quotation/Edit.js`):

```
Ext.apply(me, {
    tbar: [{
        text: 'Save',
        action: 'save'
    }]
});
```

We will install the `Save` button. Now, we want to display this button as quickly as possible, but at the moment nothing is being displayed. This is because in the card layout, in the `Quotation` view's active item, `0` will display the `List` screen and `1` will display `Edit`.

In this state, we can't perform a component test, so first, let's begin by preparing `view_edit.html` for the CT (source file: `03_making_the_quotation_form/ct/quotation/view_edit.html`).

Basically, this does not change much in `view.html`, we're just changing `view.js` being read by `<script>` in `view_edit.js`.

Now, the `Quotation` view's package name has not been amended, so you can correct this now. For the source code, please see the source file: `03_making_the_quotation_form/ct/quotation/view_edit.js`.

When you generate `MyApp.view.quotation.Quotation`, in the configuration options add `activeItem: 1`. By doing this, `Edit` will be displayed from the start. Of course the functions have not been implemented, so items will not be added or automatically calculated.

Here we are adding a new component, so in order to apply the mapping for the new component to `bootstrap.js`, let's execute `sencha app build`. After executing Sencha app build and the mapping has successfully been applied to `bootstrap.js`, the following screen should appear:

Creating the Bill form

Following on, let's make the form for invoices. The contents of the `Bill` and `Quotation` forms are mostly the same.

This will also need to describe finer details such as payment date. So, regarding the structure of the database, the ID can be linked so that a quotation can raise an event for the bill.

Now, let's quickly begin by making the card layout in the same way as for `Quotation` (source file: `04_making_the_bill_form/app/view/bill/Bill.js`):

```
Ext.define('MyApp.view.bill.Bill', {
    ...
    title: 'Bill',
    layout: 'card',
    items: [{
        xtype: 'myapp-bill-list',
        border: false
    }, {
        xtype: 'myapp-bill-edit',
        border: false
    }]
});
```

Next, let's make a temporary empty `List` component to compensate for what we wrote previously and avoid receiving an error.

The next class we are going to make is really similar to the `dashboard.Dashboard` class. So, please use that as reference while you code and watch out for the following point (source file: `04_making_the_bill_form/app/view/bill/List.js`):

```
className: MyApp.view.bill.List
extend: MyApp.form.Panel
alias: widget.myapp-bill-list
itemId: screen-bill-list
```

Also, let's implement the empty `initComponent` for the same reason as before for the `List` component.

Then, at the end, make `Edit` in the same way as `Quotation` (source file: `04_making_the_bill_form/app/view/bill/Edit.js`).

Again, this class is very similar to the `MyApp.view.quotation.Edit` class, which we previously made.

Watch out for the following points and build this class in the same way:

- className: MyApp.view.bill.Edit
- aliasName: widget.myapp-quotation-edit
- itemId: screen-quotation-edit

You have created the view, so now it's time to implement the various controllers. Instead of having one controller to manage Quotation and Bill that are separated into List and Edit, it's better to prepare controllers for each one (source file: 04_making_the_bill_form/app/controller/quotation/List.js):

```
Ext.define('MyApp.controller.quotation.List', {
    extend: 'MyApp.controller.Abstract',
    init: function() {
        var me = this;
        me.control({
        });
    }
});
```

Let's create the rest of the controllers listed as follows in exactly the same way (only the class names are different).

- (Source file: 04_making_the_bill_form/app/controller/quotation/Edit.js)
- (Source file: 04_making_the_bill_form/app/controller/bill/List.js)
- (Source file: 04_making_the_bill_form/app/controller/bill/Edit.js)

In order for the preceding controllers to be read, add a postscript into app/Application.js (source file: 04_making_the_bill_form/app/Application.js).

It's worth checking now that no errors are being displayed by accessing index.php.

Managing dirty and undirty apps

Naturally, it's good if the saving process happens every time you press the **Save** button.

However, if possible, wouldn't you prefer to have the **Save** button available only when changes have been made?

Here, we will implement the logic into the controller that will judge whether or not changes have been made after an input.

MyAccount

First, we will implement a simple form from `MyAccount`. But, before that, `Quotation` and `Bill` separated the controller, but we didn't make the change in `MyAccount`! Let's separate it quickly and add it to `app/Application.js`.

Using the `MyApp.controller.bill.Edit` class as reference, let's go ahead and make the `MyApp.controller.myaccount.Edit` class.

Apart from the class name, it's exactly the same process (source file: `05_management_of_dirty_and_undirty_myaccount/app/controller/myaccount/Edit.js`).

After you have finished building the previous class, let's add the `myaccount.Edit` controller to the controller property of `app/Application.js`.

Now add it to `app.js` in the CT directory in the same way (source file: `05_management_of_dirty_and_undirty_myaccount/ct/myaccount/app.js`).

Now, it should be able to run with a controller in CT. First, set up the following event list to fire during the component test:

- `myapp-show` (displays the component)
- `myapp-hide` (hides the component)
- `myapp-dirty` (fires when information inside the form has been changed)
- `myapp-undirty` (fires when changed information has been recorded or information has been reverted back to the previous state)

Before anything else, in relation to `myapp-show` and `myapp-hide`, we need to pass the event to the `List` and `Edit` classes with `MyApp.controller.myaccount.MyAccount` (source file: `05_management_of_dirty_and_undirty_myaccount/app/controller/myaccount/MyAccount.js`):

```
Ext.define('MyApp.controller.myaccount.MyAccount', {
    extend: 'MyApp.controller.Abstract',
    screenName: 'myaccount',
    refs: [{
        ref: 'editView', selector: 'myapp-myaccount-edit'
    }],
    init: function() {
        var me = this;
        me.control({
            'myapp-myaccount': {
                'myapp-show': me.onShow,
                'myapp-hide': me.onHide
            }
        });
    },
```

```
    onShow: function() {
        var me = this,
        editView = me.getEditView();
        editView.fireEvent('myapp-show', editView);
    },
    onHide: function() {
        var me = this,
        editView = me.getEditView();
        editView.fireEvent('myapp-hide', editView);
    }
});
```

The main point is to set up refs and capture the editView. Next, define the controller for Edit (source file: 05_management_of_dirty_and_undirty_ myaccount/app/controller/myaccount/Edit.js):

```
Ext.define('MyApp.controller.myaccount.Edit', {
extend: 'MyApp.controller.Abstract',
init: function() {
var me = this;
me.control({
            'myapp-myaccount-edit': {
                'myapp-show': me.onShow,
                'myapp-hide': me.onHide,
                'myapp-dirty': me.onDirty,
                'myapp-undirty': me.onUndirty
            }
        });
    },
    onShow: function() {
    },
    onHide: function() {
    },
    onDirty: function() {
    },
    onUndirty: function() {
    }
});
```

Next, we need to acquire the field event. Acquire the field with component query and then set up the event listener (source file: 05_management_of_dirty_and_ undirty_myaccount/app/controller/myaccount/Edit.js):

```
init: function() {
        ....
        Ext.iterate([
            {name: 'email', xtype: 'textfield', fn: me.onChangeField},
            {name: 'firstname', xtype: 'textfield', fn:
             me.onChangeField},
```

```
                    {name: 'lastname', xtype: 'textfield', fn:
                     me.onChangeField}
                ], function(f) {
                    var scope = me, o = {},
                    format = Ext.String.format,
                    key = format('{0} {1}[name="{2}"]', 'myapp-myaccount-
                    edit', f.xtype, f.name);
                    o[key] = {
        change   : { fn: f.fn, scope: scope }
                    };
                me.control(o);
                });
        },
        onChangeField: function(field) {
            console.log(field);
        },
        onShow: function() {
        ....
```

Add each name property to the View field (source file: 05_management_of_dirty_
and_undirty_myaccount/app/view/myaccount/Edit.js):

```
    Ext.define('MyApp.view.myaccount.Edit', {
        ....
        initComponent: function() {
            var me = this;
            // Fields
            Ext.apply(me, {
                ....
                items: [{
                    fieldLabel: 'email',
                    name: 'email'
                }, {
                    fieldLabel: 'firstname',
                    name: 'firstname'
                }, {
                    fieldLabel: 'lastname',
                    name: 'lastname'
                }]
            });
            ....
```

If we input something in text, it is output as a log in the console. We want to define
the similar processing to the other classes, so move the following logic into the
Abstract class and modify it so that it can be called (source file: 05_management_
of_dirty_and_undirty_myaccount/app/controller/Abstract.js):

```
    Ext.define('MyApp.controller.Abstract', {
        ....
    setChangeFieldEvents: function(fields, xtype, fn, scope) {
```

```
var me = this,
format = Ext.String.format;
Ext.iterate(fields, function(type, fs) {
if(Ext.isString(fs)) {
fs = [fs];
                }
if(Ext.isArray(fs)) {
Ext.iterate(fs, function(fname) {
var o = {}, key;
key = format('{0} {1}[name="{2}"]', xtype, type, fname);
o[key] = {
change   : { fn: fn, scope: scope }
                                };
me.control(o);
                        });
                }
        });
    },
    ....
```

And let's implement in the same way for `Edit.js` (source file: `05_management_of_dirty_and_undirty_myaccount/app/controller/myaccount/Edit.js`):

```
    ....
init: function() {
        ....
        me.setChangeFieldEvents({
            textfield: [
                'email',
                'firstname',
                'lastname'
            ]
        },
        'myapp-myaccount-edit',
        me.onChangeField,
        me);
    },
    onChangeField: function(field) {
        console.log(field);
    },
    ....
```

`setChangeFieldEvents` is made so that we can set up other events besides `textfield`. `setChangeFieldEvents` can also support the times when you want to use it for other fields such as `combobox`. The fact that the details of the text were modified means you could handle it with the implementations made so far.

So next, let's check if the content really did change. This means implementation inside the method `onChangeField` is successful.

If the content of the component recorded by the `MyApp.controller.myaccount.Edit` controller's `init` method is modified, the `onChangeField` method is implemented (source file: `05_management_of_dirty_and_undirty_myaccount/app/controller/myaccount/Edit.js`).

Use `getFieldValues` in order to judge whether there were changes to the field. `Ext.Object.getKeys` will send back an array. Consequently, with this single line you can judge whether changes have been made to the content.

If there is a change, `myapp-dirty` will be fired and if it reverts to its original state, the `myapp-undirty` event will be fired.

So, let's add the logic to make the toolbar button available for `onDirty` and unavailable for `onUndirty` to finish the implementation of `MyAccount` (source file: `05_management_of_dirty_and_undirty_myaccount/app/controller/myaccount/Edit.js`):

```
Ext.define('MyApp.controller.myaccount.Edit', {
    ....
    onDirty: function() {
        var me = this,
        editView = me.getEditView(),
        btnSave = editView.down('button[action=save]')
        btnSave.enable();
    },
    onUndirty: function() {
        var me = this,
        editView = me.getEditView(),
        btnSave = editView.down('button[action=save]')
        btnSave.disable();
    }
});
```

Let's add `disabled` to the `Save` button settings. During the CT error, `onShow` does not work. Also, you should conduct the button's initialization when it is `onHide` (source file: `05_management_of_dirty_and_undirty_myaccount/app/view/myaccount/Edit.js`):

```
Ext.define('MyApp.view.myaccount.Edit', {
    ....
    tbar: [{
        text: 'Save',
        action: 'save',
        disabled: true
    ....
```

Finally, if you can muster enough energy, implement it so that when the reset button is pressed, the reset method is called from `Ext.form.Basic`.

The Quotation form

The `Quotation` form is mostly the same as `Bill` and `MyAccount`, but there is one big difference — there is a grid inside the form panel.

At first glance, the store that is configured to the `grid` panel looks as though it will communicate directly with the server, but this is not the case. To the very end, this form panel handles fields, so it doesn't handle the grid directly and there is no need to separate form data sending and grid data sending.

Then how do we solve this? The answer is to hand it a hidden field and make it save the grid data in the form of JSON. So, the grid store is fine to be left as a **MemoryStore**.

First, implement it to the same point as `MyAccount`. Because `Quotation` will hold a list, add to it so that `refs` can also acquire a list view.

This source code is very similar to the implementation from the previous step of the following classes:

- `MyApp.controller.myaccount.MyAccount`
- `MyApp.controller.myaccount.Edit`

Try implementing for `Quotation` remembering what we did with the source code from the previous classes. Use the following source files for reference if you get stuck:

- `06_management_of_dirty_and_undirty_quotation/app/controller/quotation/Quotation.js`
- `06_management_of_dirty_and_undirty_quotation/app/controller/quotation/Edit.js`

In order to check the application you have implemented so far, add a CT to check `Edit` (source file: `06_management_of_dirty_and_undirty_quotation/ct/quotation/app_edit.html`).

We'll make this anew in the CT directory subsidiary. The content is mostly the same as for `app.html`, but we will change what will be read from `app.js` to `app_edit.js` (source file: `06_management_of_dirty_and_undirty_quotation/ct/quotation/app_edit.js`).

This is also almost the same as `app.js` on the same tier, but we'll add an `Edit` controller to controllers and `activeItem:1` to `QuotationView` controller's configuration option.

The main points to remember are to add `quotation.Edit` to the controller and set `activeItem` to `1` and display the `Edit` panel from the beginning. So, like we touched on initially, take the store data that's configured in `grid` and make it into JSON, then create the logic to be stored in the `Hidden` field. First, we need to lay out the `Hidden` field in `view` (source file: `06_management_of_dirty_and_undirty_quotation/app/view/quotation/Edit.js`):

```
Ext.define('MyApp.view.quotation.Edit', {
            ....
            }, {
            name: 'items',
            xtype: 'hidden'
            }, {
            fieldLabel: 'note',
            name: 'note',
            xtype: 'textarea',
            width: 500
            }]
        });
        // TopToolbar
```

In this state, the data is fixed and cannot obtain an event that has specifically changed. Before this, let's implement the addition and deletion of items and event editing. There are various things we need to do to achieve that.

First is to change the `Store` component into a class. You just need to take what is already generated inside `view` and make it into an external class (source file: `06_management_of_dirty_and_undirty_quotation/app/store/Customer.js`):

```
Ext.define('MyApp.store.Customer',{
    extend: 'Ext.data.Store',
    storeId:'Customer',
    fields: ['id', 'name'],
    data:{'items':[
        {"id": 0, "name": "Sencha"},
        {"id": 1, "name": "Xenophy"}
    ]},
proxy: {
    type: 'memory',
    reader: {
        type: 'json',
        root: 'items'
        }
    }
});
```

Also, change the following (source file: 06_management_of_dirty_and_undirty_ quotation/app/store/QuotationItem.js):

```
Ext.define('MyApp.store.QuotationItem',{
    extend: 'Ext.data.Store',
    storeId:'QuotationItem',
    fields:['desc', 'qty', 'price', 'sum'],
    data:{'items':[
    ]},
proxy: {
    ... // Customer Store
    }
});
```

In order to use this store class, add the setting to the MyApp.controller. quotation.Edit class.

We'll add Customer and QuotationItem to the MyApp.controller.quotation. Edit class's stores property (source file: 06_management_of_dirty_and_undirty_ quotation/app/controller/quotation/Edit.js).

Because we have created MyApp.store.Customer and MyApp.store.QuotationItem outside of view, we need to adjust the code in view (source file: 06_management_of_ dirty_and_undirty_quotation/app/view/quotation/Edit.js):

```
Ext.define('MyApp.view.quotation.Edit', {
        ....
        (remove store defines!!)
        ....
        // Fields & Grid
Ext.apply(me, {
    bodyPadding: 20,
    items: [{
            ....
    store: 'Customer',
            ....
            }, {
                // Grid Panel
                ....
            store: 'QuotationItem',
                ....
```

There is a reason why we externalized store. This is because if we configure the store class in stores with **Ext JS MVC architecture**, the getXXXXStore method is generated and we're then able to access the store component from the controller. XXXX is the store class name.

Next, we will make modifications to monitor changes to `hidden` from the controller and change the initial values to `hidden` (source file: `06_management_of_dirty_and_undirty_quotation/app/view/quotation/Edit.js`):

```
name: 'items',
xtype: 'hidden',
value: '[]'
```

Also, change the following code (source file: `06_management_of_dirty_and_undirty_quotation/app/controller/quotation/Edit.js`):

```
me.setChangeFieldEvents({
combo: [
        'customer'
    ],
hidden: [
        'items'
    ],
textarea: [
        'note'
    ]
},
```

Finally, we can implement what operates the grid. First define the event handler for the button (source file: `06_management_of_dirty_and_undirty_quotation/app/controller/quotation/Edit.js`).

Implement `onAddItem` and `onRemoveItem`. Here it will become possible to add items and delete items on the grid (source file: `06_management_of_dirty_and_undirty_quotation/app/controller/quotation/Edit.js`):

```
onAddItem: function() {
    var me = this,
    store = me.getQuotationItemStore();
    store.add({ desc: 'New Item', qty: 0, price: 0, sum: 0 });
},
onRemoveItem: function() {
    var me = this,
    store = me.getQuotationItemStore();
    editView = me.getEditView(),
    grid = editView.down('grid'),
    sm = grid.getSelectionModel();
    if(sm.getCount()) {
            var next = false;
            Ext.iterate(sm.getSelection(), function(item) {
        var flg = false;
        store.data.each(function(model) {
                if(flg) {
                next = model;
```

```
                    flg = false;
                    }
            if(model.id === item.id) {
                    flg = true;
                    }
            });
            store.remove(item);
        });
        if(next) {
            sm.select(next);
        } else {
            next = store.getAt(store.data.getCount() - 1);
            if(next) {
                sm.select(next);
            }
        }
    }
},
```

The adding process is extremely simple, it's just using the Add method from the store and adding records. However, the deletion process is not just simply deleting.

It has been set so that when deletion occurs, the next item from the one that was selected comes into being, and that item is selected. By doing this, you can keep deleting just by continuing to click on the **Delete** button. You should think of this as a little bonus feature!

So, now you can add and delete records on the grid. Next, we will implement the essential part that turns the store data into JSON and stores it in hidden (source file: 06_management_of_dirty_and_undirty_quotation/app/controller/quotation/Edit.js):

```
Ext.define('MyApp.controller.quotation.Edit', {
    ....
    init: function() {
        ....
        var store = me.getQuotationItemStore(),
        updateGridData;
        updateGridData = function(store) {
          var f = me.getEditView().query('hidden[name=items]')[0],
          out = [];
          store.data.each(function(r) {
              out.push(Ext.clone(r.data));
            });
          f.setValue(Ext.encode(out));
        };
        store.on('update', function(store, r) {
          r.set('sum', r.get('qty')*r.get('price'));
          updateGridData(store);
```

```
      });
      store.on('add', function(store, r) {
        updateGridData(store);
      });
      store.on('remove', function(store, r) {
        updateGridData(store);
      });
    },
```

When the grid data is altered, update, add, and remove occur as a separate events. You need to define these event handlers. The process is common, so first store the function object in updateGridData and then use it.

Again implement a bonus function for the update event. When the content is modified, multiply qty and price and then it will place the value automatically inside sum. This time it's made so you can't edit sum, it's set to input after calculating automatically. You can check that it works at ct/quotation/app_edit.html.

Until now we have been defining stores in View. However, because we changed the stores into class files, you might have noticed that ct/ quotation/view_edit.html isn't working properly. At the end of Quotation, let's make modifications so that the CT will work normally (source file: 06_management_of_dirty_and_undirty_quotation/ct/quotation/view_edit.js):

```
Ext.onReady(function() {
    Ext.create('MyApp.store.Customer');
    Ext.create('MyApp.store.QuotationItem');
    Ext.create('MyApp.view.quotation.Quotation', {
      activeItem: 1,
      width: 800,
      height: 600,
      renderTo: Ext.getBody()
    });
});
```

Because there is no controller, the creation of the store component will not occur. Due to this, if you define and generate it yourself, it will be linked with storeId and then displayed. Of course, nothing will happen if you press any of the buttons displayed because there is no controller.

The implementation of Quotation has been longer and more complicated than anything preceding it. Next is Bill, which is more or less the same implementation. Please double-check the complex parts as you go.

The Bill form

As we know, `Bill` is pretty much the same as `Quotation`, but let's continue and implement `Bill`. First let's make the `BillItem` store class.

For `Bill`, it's only the class name and `StoreId` that differs from `QuotationItem`. The rest is the same, so let's try and code this by ourselves. You can check out the following source file if you want something to refer to:

`07_management_of_dirty_and_undirty_bill/app/store/BillItem.js`

Next comes the controller setting. Again, the following implementations are extremely similar to what came before in `Quotation`, so think back to `MyApp.controller.quotation.Quotation` and `MyApp.controller.quotation.Edit` and try it for yourself. If you need help, you can find the source files at the following:

- `07_management_of_dirty_and_undirty_bill/app/controller/bill/Bill.js`
- `07_management_of_dirty_and_undirty_bill/app/controller/bill/Edit.js`

Finally, lets modifying `view`. In the same way, this is very similar to `EditView`, so think back to `MyApp.view.quotation.Edit` and try it for yourself. The following is the source file if you need some help:

`07_management_of_dirty_and_undirty_bill/app/view/bill/Edit.js`

Let's modify and add the CT. In the same way as the previous step, in order to validate the `EditView`, we will build `app.html` and `view.html` afresh for `Edit`.

What is happening internally is mostly the same, so please refer to the following source files:

- `07_management_of_dirty_and_undirty_bill/ct/bill/app_edit.html`
- `07_management_of_dirty_and_undirty_bill/ct/bill/app_edit.js`
- `07_management_of_dirty_and_undirty_bill/ct/bill/view_edit.html`
- `07_management_of_dirty_and_undirty_bill/ct/bill/view_edit.js`

Regarding `app_edit.js`, in order for mutual validation to occur with the controller, we install a button on the screen and make an event fire.

If no errors come up with CT or in the whole application, move to the next section.

Implementing the read and write processes using Ext Direct

From here, we will start to implement the processing of data being written and read concerning the form that we have made this far. We'll be using Ext Direct for this as well. Before we continue with the following implementation, there are a few points that you should amend. One of those is to add an **ID** to a session when you log in. Let's amend this now (source file: `08_implement_read_and_write_by_ext_direct/index.php`):

```
....
"SELECT",
"    COUNT(id) as auth,",
"    users.id,", // <- add
"    users.email,",
....
```

Then, store the session ID:

```
....
$_SESSION["USERINFO"] = array(
    "id" => $row["id"], // <- add
    "email" => $row["email"],
    ....
```

Next, add `session_start` to the beginning of the router being used by Ext Direct. By doing this, you should be able to access the session with the method from each class (source file: `08_implement_read_and_write_by_ext_direct/php/router.php`).

```
<?php
session_start(); // <-- add
require('config.php');
```

You have prepared the way, so now let's go ahead and implement the read process for `MyAccount`, `Quotation`, and `Bill`.

Reading data

Here, we will start to learn about how the various sections of our application will read data.

MyAccount

To begin with, let's start working on `MyAccount`. Let's create a class for Ext Direct. Here we will add the source code for a new PHP.

Because the source code is going to be a little long to be added to this text, please refer to your source file at: `09_reading_data_myaccount/php/classes/MyAppMyAccount.php`.

Implement the `readForm` method. When a person logs in, it acquires the account information from the database by using the saved ID as a reference.

I'll hold back from explaining the PHP processing that happens around here. The main point is the returned associative array key.

The access key is a flag that gives the value `true` or `false` indicating whether the form's acquisition was successful or not. The data for each field is configured as an associative array in the data key. In order to use this `readForm` in Ext Direct, update the `REMOTING_API` output configurations.

We will add a new class for Direct (source file: `09_reading_data_myaccount/php/config.php`):

```
'MyAppMyAccount' =>array(
    'methods' => array(
        'readForm' => array(
            'len' => 0
        )
    )
)
```

Now there is just a bit more preparation to be done. The CT of `MyAccount` is not preset to use Ext Direct, so we should amend this. First, add `api.php` to the HTML. In order to make our database read `api.php` just before reading `app.js`, we need to add the following code (source file: `09_reading_data_myaccount/ct/myaccount/app.html`):

```
<script src="../../php/api.php"></script>
```

Next, add the Ext Direct setting to `app.js`. Let's add the following code after `Ext.Loader.setConfig` (source file: `09_reading_data_myaccount/ct/myaccount/app.js`):

```
Ext.app.REMOTING_API.url = "../../php/router.php";
Ext.direct.Manager.addProvider(Ext.app.REMOTING_API);
```

The `Ext.app.REMOTING_API.url` file is being created by `api.php` that is being read by `app.html`. At this point, the URL path is different for the CT, so you should override this. Now we've finally prepared everything, so let's go on and set up Ext Direct in the `MyAccount` form (`view`).

We'll add an `api` property to `MyApp.ciew.myaccount.Edit` (source file: 09_reading_data_myaccount/app/view/myaccount/Edit.js):

```
Ext.define('MyApp.view.myaccount.Edit', {
    ....
    api: {
      load      : 'MyAppMyAccount.readForm',
      submit    : 'MyAppMyAccount.writeForm'
```

Set up the object in the `config.php` file named `API`. Specify `load` and `submit` inside that key. Set up the character string for the `Ext.Direct` function in the same way in which both `load` and `submit` methods specified their class name in the character string in `Ext.create` and `Ext.define`.

Now, because `MyAccount` wants to read when it is `onShow` (when it's displayed), the `myapp-show` event in the CT doesn't fire. So, let's install this button that will cause a pseudo-fire event.

In the CT subsidiary directory, because we will add a button that's necessary for the fake reproduction of `myapp-show`, we need to add the following code inside the `launch` method (source file: 09_reading_data_myaccount/ct/myaccount/app.js):

```
Ext.widget('button', {
text: 'fire myapp-show',
renderTo: Ext.getBody(),
scope: this,
handler: function() {
        this.getController('myaccount.MyAccount')
        .loadIndex('#!/myaccount');
        }
    });
```

We can make the `myapp-show` event mock fire by forcefully implementing a structure that automatically calls the `loadIndex` method that we made a while back. So if you press the button, you can make the event fire. Now, implement the read logic for the form data in the `onShow` method.

Finally, we will implement the controller behavior after `myapp-show` fires (source file: 09_reading_data_myaccount/app/controller/myaccount/Edit.js):

```
onShow: function(p, owner, params) {
    var me = this,
    editView = me.getEditView(),
```

```
    form = editView.getForm();

    p.setLoading();
    form.trackResetOnLoad = true;
    form.isLoading = true;
    form.load({
      success: function(form, ret) {
        p.setLoading(false);
        p.fireEvent('myapp-undirty');
        form.isLoading = false;
        }
    });
  },
```

It was a fairly short code. The main point is to acquire the `BasicForm` object with `getForm` and to set `trackResetOnLoad` to `true`.

We can use `isLoading` to judge a situation when other processing happens while it is asynchronously reading. If we call the `load` method, the object we configured before in the API key is executed and the request is sent to the server. PHP acquires the data from the database and sends it back, and the variable is inserted automatically in the field. We don't need to go through the process of setting the data we receive into the field ourselves.

After the `MyAccount` controller has finished reading the login information, as it's the latest user information, the `myapp-undirty` event fires. From then on, the **Save** button can now be pressed if there is a modification. Later, we'll implement a part that will send the data in reverse when the **Save** button is pressed.

The Quotation form

Now let's implement the read action in for the `Quotation` form. First, set up the Ext Direct in the CT.

In the same way as we added to `MyAccount`, we will add the following code to `app_edit.js` (source file: `10_reading_data_quotation/ct/quotation/app_edit.js`):

```
Ext.app.REMOTING_API.url = "../../php/router.php";
Ext.direct.Manager.addProvider(Ext.app.REMOTING_API);
```

Don't forget to read the API key, so let's set this up now.

In the same way as we did on the HTML side, make it read the `api.php` file to make use of Direct. If you need a reminder, see the source file at `10_reading_data_quotation/ct/quotation/app_edit.html`.

Next, we'll do the preparations on the server side. Like you understood up until now, the process is mostly the same as with MyAccount.

We will add a new API key for Quotation to config.php (source file: 10_reading_data_quotation/ct/quotation/app_edit.js):

```
'MyAppQuotation'=>array(
    'methods'=>array(
        'readForm'=>array(
            'len'=>0
        ),
        'writeForm'=>array(
            'len'=>1,
            'formHandler'=>true
        )
    )
),
'MyAppMyAccount'=>array(
    ....
)
```

Next, implement the class you defined with config.php. We are going to implement the API key we added to config.php.

For the content, please see the following source file for reference:

10_reading_data_quotation/php/classes/MyAppQuotation.php

Implement the readForm method. With the writeForm method, in the case of Quotation, if the complex process to judge whether it is an update or a new addition becomes necessary, in order to judge whether it has an ID or not from the transition that's listed, it can't be implemented in this chapter, so implement it in the next chapter. This is the same with Bill.

So, in order to communicate by using the class on the server side, define the setting in the config API in the form panel.

We will define the API property in the same way as we did for the MyApp.view.myaccount.Edit class (source file: 10_reading_data_quotation/app/view/quotation/Edit.js).

Define the myapp-show event handler. This will be quite a long source code. So, while being careful to look out for the new and edit points inside the onShow method, try it out by using the following source file for reference:

10_reading_data_quotation/app/controller/quotation/Edit.js

The functions have been divided into onEditShow and onNewShow. This time, only onEditShow method will run. With a later-listed implementation, newly made processes and the processes that are divided after editing are also implemented.

After it has finished reading, fire myapp-undirty in order to know whether it is in a clean condition. The button to fire the myapp-show event is already installed in the CT, so if you press the button, it will signal and begin to read.

Of course it's the processing of the readForm method, so it's only the fixed test data that will be read. But we can implement the reading from the database with SQL along with the implementation of writeForm that happens in the next chapter. With the name specified on the server side, we need to set a name in the field on the client side. If the name is correctly set up, the data should be inserted automatically.

The Bill form

Finally, implement Bill in the same way as Quotation. Firstly, configure Ext Direct in the CT.

Like in the previous step, we will add the code necessary for Direct (source file: 11_reading_data_bill/ct/bill/app_edit.js).

Configure it without forgetting about reading the API key. This also repeats the process of making the HTML read api.php (source file: 11_reading_data_bill/ct/bill/app_edit.html).

Now prepare the server side. We will add the API class for Direct that's used by the Bill class (source file: 11_reading_data_bill/php/config.php):

```
'MyAppBill'=>array(
    'methods'=>array(
        'readForm'=>array(
            'len'=>0
        ),
        'writeForm'=>array(
            'len'=>1,
            'formHandler'=>true
        )
    )
),
'MyAppQuotation'=>array(
```

Next, implement the class defined by config.php.

Because the code is very long, please refer to the following source file on this occasion:

`11_reading_data_bill/php/classes/MyAppBill.php`

Then, configure the direct function in the API config file. Let's define the API property in the same way as we did for the `MyApp.view.quotation.Edit` class (source file: `11_reading_data_bill/app/view/bill/Edit.js`).

Finally, implement the event handler `myapp-show`. This is really similar to the implementation of `MyApp.controller.quotation.Edit`, so please try it for yourself. If you need to, you can refer to the source file at `11_reading_data_bill/app/view/bill/Edit.js`.

Writing data and validations

In regard to the writing process, as I mentioned before, just implement `MyAccount` and implement `writeForm` of `MyAccount`.

This is also quite long, so please refer to the source file `12_writing_data_and_validations/php/classes/MyAppMyAccount.php`.

The content of the process is simple; however, if you look at the PHP code, it looks pretty complicated. I'll try to explain it simply.

First, to return the associative array as a return value in the same way as the others, we have to set `success` as `true` and relay to the client that the writing process has finished normally.

At the beginning, there are places where we set the associative array with a key called `errors`, then set a field name key inside and insert a message. This is the input check on the server side.

If you use Ext Direct, this completes the input check.

Under errors, put in the field name for the error target and just by entering the error message in there, the server side automatically displays a red frame. If you hover the mouse over it, the message you set up on the server side is displayed. In other words, you need zero lines of programming code on the client side for error processing.

Normally, you receive the JSON data by communicating through AJAX, but we need to define the error processing on the client side and the server side. So, I'm sure we would all prefer to use Ext Direct, which automatically processes this for us.

 If you get used to this way of developing, you'll get hooked and you won't be able to go back.

Again, because you can wholly separate the client side and server side, one engineer does not need to construct both. Instead, it's possible to progress the work by completely separating the server side and client side. Once the input check has been passed, the user information is acquired from the database where the session ID is being saved.

Finally, set up the success key that displays `true` when the processing has been completed. `writeForm` is an implemented method used when writing form data. In the member on the server side that writes the form data, you need to set the `formHandler` method to `true`.

Everyone already has `formHandler` in `config.php` set to `true`, but when you get down to defining your own projects in a similar way, people often encounter problems when they forget to set the `formHandler` method to `true` meaning the data is not sent.

 Set the `formHandler` method to `true`.

Summary

Great work so far! This was quite a long chapter, but this was also integral to our application (yes, all the chapters are integral, but this one more so!).

In this chapter, we started with the login screen and then implemented the `Edit` screen that uses forms from each screen. At the end, we learnt about Ext Direct.

In the next chapter, we'll implement the `List` and `Search` functions for each screen that uses Ext Direct. Have a quick coffee break and carry on when you're ready!

4
List and Search

In previous chapters we looked at preparing the data structure and the basic Ext JS architecture, and in *Chapter 3, Data Input*, we looked at inputting data. However, we couldn't implement the writing of the data from the `Quotation` form. This was because we couldn't judge whether it was a new addition or an editing process due to listing being non-existent.

When you actually construct an application, it is probably most common to build the list first and then create the form. However, this time we learned to read the form first and then save it. So, just choose whichever way you find easier to build with.

This chapter is mainly about displaying data that was read in the previous chapter. However, users will no doubt want to search for data, so we will also learn about data searches.

In this chapter you will learn how to:

- Get data from the database
- Apply the acquired data to the store
- Connect the store and the grid
- Read data to fields
- Search the list

Creating the Quotation list

So, let's straightaway start with preparing the CT to create the Quotation list. We will create view_list.htm and view_list.js (source file: 01_creating_ quotation_list/ct/quotation/view_list.html).

The view_list.html file is a reproduction of other view files, and so inside the internal reading, change the .js file in the view that's being read to view_list.js (source file: 01_creating_quotation_list/ct/quotation/view_list.js).

The view_list.js file is also almost similar. It's only a little bit different.

```
Ext.onReady(function() {
    Ext.create('MyApp.store.Customer');
    Ext.create('MyApp.store.QuotationItem');
    Ext.create('MyApp.store.Quotation');
    Ext.create('MyApp.view.quotation.Quotation', {
        activeItem: 0,
    ...
```

By now, preparing the CT should have become a straightforward process.

Unlike edit, set the activeItem in the list to 0. If you check how it looks in a browser, only the Quotation panel will be displayed.

Let's begin to build the inside.

Creating the Quotation model

First, you want to build a store, but let's build a model before that (source file: 02_creating_quotation_model/app/model/Quotation.js).

Let's implement the Quotation model class that has a newly acquired id, customer, modified and created.

Define the id, customer name, modified date/time, and created date/time parameters. Then, we'll implement the store that was used in the model in the previous step (source file: 02_creating_quotation_model/app/store/Quotation.js).

```
Ext.define('MyApp.store.Quotation', {
    extend: 'Ext.data.Store',
    storeId: 'QuotationList',
    model: 'MyApp.model.Quotation',
    remoteSort: true,
    pageSize: 100,
    proxy: {
        type: 'direct',
```

```
            directFn: 'MyAppQuotation.getGrid',
            reader: {
                type: 'json',
                root: 'items',
                totalProperty: 'total'
            }
        }
    });
```

Specify `MyAppQuotation.getGrid` in `directFn`. This is the method name where the store is going to acquire the data. Of course, this is a new construction. In other words, add a method to the PHP class and with what you have experienced so far, you should easily be able to imagine whether it's necessary to add `config.php`.

So, first implement the method even though it is empty (source file: `02_creating_quotation_model/php/classes/MyAppQuotation.php`).

There is one argument and for this a search condition will be sent from the store (source file: `02_creating_quotation_model/php/config.php`).

```
<?php
$API = array(
    ....
    'MyAppQuotation'=>array(
        'methods'=>array(
            ....
            'getGrid'=>array(
                'len'=>1
            )
        )
    ),
    ....
);
```

Updating the Quotation view

You've prepared everything for the grid to be displayed, so let's implement the view (source file: `03_update_the_quotation_view/app/view/quotation/List.js`):

```
Ext.define('MyApp.view.quotation.List', {
    ...
    initComponent: function() {
        var me = this;
        Ext.apply(me, {
            columns: [{
                text: 'Customer',
                dataIndex: 'customer',
                flex: 1
```

```
            }, {
                text: 'Modified',
                dataIndex: 'modified',
                width: 120
            }, {
                text: 'Created',
                dataIndex: 'created',
                width: 120
            }]
        });
        me.callParent(arguments);
    }
});
```

Here you are only specifying columns. In order to abstract the grid panel, we are creating the `MyApp.grid.Panel` class. (source file: `03_update_the_quotation_view/app/grid/Panel.js`).

We will create the `MyApp.grid.Panel` class that is purely inherited from the `Ext.grid.Panel` class.

We have just simply succeeded the `Ext.grid.Panel` class. That's pretty much what abstraction is. Now, it should look like the following if you display it:

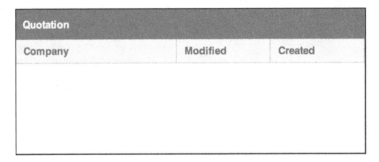

It has been a while since we saw an image, so we've displayed a column for now; however, let's start to create the necessary objects for this list.

The next thing to add is the toolbar with buttons. Let's go ahead and add the following buttons (source file: `03_update_the_quotation_view/app/view/quotation/List.js`):

- Add
- Edit
- Delete
- Update

This can be implemented using the following code:

```
Ext.define('MyApp.view.quotation.List', {
    ....
    initComponent: function() {
        var me = this;
        Ext.apply(me, {
            tbar: [{
                text: 'Add',
                disabled: true,
                action: 'add'
            }, {
                text     : 'Edit',
                disabled : true,
                action   : 'edit'
            }, {
                text     : 'Remove',
                disabled : true,
                action   : 'remove'
            }, '-', {
                text     : 'Refresh',
                disabled : true,
                action   : 'refresh'
            }]
        });
    ....
```

We have installed the buttons, so now describe the event handler that deals with this to the controller (source file: `03_update_the_quotation_view/app/controller/quotation/List.js`).

In the control for the `MyApp.controller.quotation.List` class, use the following selectors and register each handler with the `click` event (at the same time we'll implement each empty handler):

- For selector: `'myapp-quotation-list button[action=add]'` use handler: `onItemAdd`

- For selector: `'myapp-quotation-list button[action=edit]'` use handler: `onItemEdit`

- For selector: `'myapp-quotation-list button[action=remove]'` use handler: `onItemRemove`

- For selector: `'myapp-quotation-list button[action=refresh]'` use handler: `onStoreRefresh`

If you want to check whether the event responds or not, you can set `disabled` to `false`, or reset it and then check the performance. We'll create an implementation later so that the status of the disable button changes according to whether the list has been selected or not.

Next, let's implement `SearchField` for searches. We'll place this in the top toolbar we created earlier. But before you can do that, you'll need to implement `SearchField`. The `SearchField` is distributed from the beginning as `ux`, but this time we'll use this as a reference to construct anew (source file: `03_update_the_quotation_view/app/form/SearchField.js`).

```
Ext.define('MyApp.form.SearchField', {
    extend: 'Ext.form.field.Trigger',
    alias: 'widget.myapp-searchfield',
    trigger1Cls: Ext.baseCSSPrefix + 'form-clear-trigger',
    trigger2Cls: Ext.baseCSSPrefix + 'form-search-trigger',
    hasSearch : false,
    paramName : 'query',
    initComponent: function() {
        var me = this;
        me.callParent(arguments);
        me.on('specialkey', function(f, e){
            if(e.getKey() == e.ENTER) {
                me.onTrigger2Click();
            }
        });
    },
    afterRender: function() {
        this.callParent();
        this.triggerCell.item(0).setDisplayed(false);
    },
    onTrigger1Click : function() {
        var me = this;
        if(me.hasSearch) {
            me.setValue('');
            me.hasSearch = false;
            me.triggerCell.item(0).setDisplayed(false);
            location.href = me.urlRoot;
        }
    },
    onTrigger2Click : function() {
        var me = this,
            value = me.getValue();
        if(value.length > 0) {
            me.triggerCell.item(0).setDisplayed(true);
```

```
        location.href = Ext.String.format('{0}q={1}', me.urlRoot,
        value);
    }
  }
});
```

Next, add the paging toolbar. Install it along with SearchField. Displaying 100 to
1,000 items at a time would be optimal. In order to declare the use of SearchField,
set MyApp.form.SearchField in requires (source file: 03_update_the_quotation_
view/app/view/quotation/List.js).

```
    ....
    initComponent: function() {
        var me = this;
        Ext.apply(me, {
            tbar: [{
                ....
            }, '->', {
                xtype    : 'myapp-searchfield',
                disabled : true,
                width    : 150
            }],
            bbar: {
                xtype       : 'pagingtoolbar',
                displayInfo : true
            }
    ....
```

Finally, let's slightly customize the grid. Modify the SelectionModel and then
make the selection possible with a checkbox. We'll install this so it offers a
user interface that lets you delete items collectively. To do this, you'll use Ext.
selection.CheckboxModel (source file: 03_update_the_quotation_view/app/
view/quotation/List.js).

```
Ext.define('MyApp.view.quotation.List', {
    ....
    requires: [
        'MyApp.form.SearchField',
        'Ext.selection.CheckboxModel'
    ],
    initComponent: function() {
        var me = this;
        Ext.apply(me, {
            selModel: Ext.create('Ext.selection.CheckboxModel')
        });
        Ext.apply(me, {
            tbar: [{
                text: 'Add',
                ....
```

In the same way as with `SearchField`, define the reading of `Ext.selection.CheckboxModel` in requires. Again, regarding the `selModel`, set the `Ext.selection.CheckboxModel` instance. If you finish configuring it all, it should look like this:

Implementing the Quotation controller

It's starting to look like the real thing! So, now let's implement the part that will actually read and display the data. First, as usual, start with the implementation of the CT (source file: `04_implement_quotation_controller/ct/quotation/view_list.html`).

Reproduce `app_edit.html` and change the `.js` file that is being read to `app_list.js`. Again, be careful because we'll read the `api.php` file together (source file: `04_implement_quotation_controller/ct/quotation/view_list.js`).

```
...
Ext.application({
    ...
    controllers: [
        'quotation.Quotation',
        'quotation.Edit',
        'quotation.List'
    ],
    launch: function() {
        var panel = Ext.create('MyApp.view.quotation.Quotation', {
            width: 800,
            height: 600,
            activeItem: 0,
            renderTo: Ext.getBody()
```

```
        });
        Ext.util.Observable.capture(panel, function() {
            console.log(arguments);
        });
        Ext.widget('button', {
            text: 'fire myapp-show',
            renderTo: Ext.getBody(),
            scope: this,
            handler: function() {
                this.getController('quotation.Quotation')
                .loadIndex('#!/quotation');
            }
        });
    }
});
```

Be aware that the `direct` setup is also underway.

Now prepare the button that mock fires the `myapp-show` event. Of course we will also add the `List` controller (source file: `04_implement_quotation_controller/ app/controller/quotation/List.js`).

Here, we'll add the `myapp-show` event to `stores`, `refs`, `myapp-quotationlist`, and finally we'll implement the `onShow` method:

```
Ext.define('MyApp.controller.quotation.List', {
    extend: 'MyApp.controller.Abstract',
    stores: [
        'Quotation'
    ],
    refs: [{
        ref: 'listView', selector: 'myapp-quotation-list'
    }],
    init: function() {
        var me = this;
        me.control({
            'myapp-quotation-list': {
                'myapp-show': me.onShow
            },
    ...
    },
    onShow: function(p, owner, params) {
        var me          = this,
            listView    = me.getListView(),
            btnAdd      = listView.down('button[action=add]'),
            btnEdit     = listView.down('button[action=edit]'),
            btnRemove   = listView.down('button[action=remove]'),
            btnRefresh  = listView.down('button[action=refresh]'),
            fieldSearch = listView.down('myapp-searchfield'),
            query       = params.q;
```

```
            btnAdd.disable();
            btnEdit.disable();
            btnRemove.disable();
            btnRefresh.disable();
            if(query) {
                fieldSearch.setValue(query);
                fieldSearch.triggerCell.item(0).setDisplayed(true);
                fieldSearch.hasSearch = true;
            }
            fieldSearch.urlRoot = '#!/quotation/';
            fieldSearch.disable();
            listView.getStore().load({
                params: {
                    query: query
                },
                callback: function(records, operation, success) {
                    btnAdd.enable();
                    btnRefresh.enable();
                    fieldSearch.enable();
                }
            });
        },
        ...
});
```

Add the event handler and then implement the onShow event. Acquire the list view from the store and call the load method.

In order to acquire the list view and store, make sure that stores and refs are configured. This time, we will also amend the component side, that is, the view side (source File: 04_implement_quotation_controller/app/view/quotation/ List.js).

```
Ext.define('MyApp.view.quotation.List', {
    ....
    initComponent: function() {
        var me = this,
            store = me.getStore();
        if(!store) {
            store = Ext.create('MyApp.store.Quotation');
            me.store = store;
        }
        Ext.apply(me, {
        ....
```

Set up the `store` object in the `initComponent` method. Run the CT and if you press the button, the store will use the `DirectFn` method that was set up and transmissions will occur. Of course the server-side implementation has not happened, so nothing will be displayed in the list.

Loading the grid and implementing toolbar buttons

Generally speaking, a grid is not a grid if it can't read data. For the time being, let's just read the data from the database and display it in the grid (source file: `05_loading_the_grid_and_implementing_toolbar_buttons/php/classes/MyAppQuotation.php`).

Here we'll implement the `getGrid` method for `MyAppQuotation.php` that was returning empty data.

 The code for this is a little bit long, so please refer to the source file to see the code.

If we put any old data in the database it will be displayed. But, because the items we want to display have increased slightly, we need to amend the JavaScript source code. Add the two files `addr` and `note` to the `Quotation` model (source file: `05_loading_the_grid_and_implementing_toolbar_buttons/app/model/Quotation.js`).

Now let's add the two files we added in the previous step to the `columns` property in `MyApp.view.quotation.List` (source file: `05_loading_the_grid_and_implementing_toolbar_buttons/app/view/quotation/List.js`):

```
    . . .
            }, {
                text: 'Address',
                dataIndex: 'addr',
                flex: 1
            }, {
                text: 'Note',
                dataIndex: 'note',
                flex: 1
            }, {
    . . .
```

We have added the `addr`, `modified`, and `created` files. The data is random but columns are displayed, and the data is read as in the following screenshot:

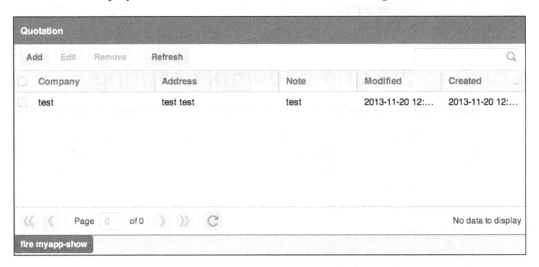

Next comes the building of registration processes, something we left undone in *Chapter 3*, *Data Input*. In order to do that, first implement the event handler for the toolbar buttons and then display the **Add New** and **Editing** screens (source file: `05_loading_the_grid_and_implementing_toolbar_buttons/app/controller/quotation/List.js`).

```
Ext.define('MyApp.controller.quotation.List', {
    ....
    onItemAdd: function() {
        var me            = this,
            listView      = me.getListView();
        listView.fireEvent('myapp-add');
    },
```

Fire the `myapp-add` event in the list view component (source file: `05_loading_the_grid_and_implementing_toolbar_buttons/app/controller/quotation/Quotation.js`).

```
Ext.define('MyApp.controller.quotation.Quotation', {
    ....
    init: function() {
        var me = this,
            format = Ext.String.format;
        me.control({
            'myapp-quotation-list': {
                'myapp-add': function() {
                    location.href = format('#!/{0}/new',
                    me.screenName);
```

```
            }
        },
    ....
```

Then describe the `myapp-add` event handler in the `MyApp.controller.quotation.`
`Quotation` class. Here, specify the URL in `location.href` and then move the screen.
Not in a CT, but if you display the whole application in `index.php`, you should be
able to check the way the screen changes when you click on the **Add** button.

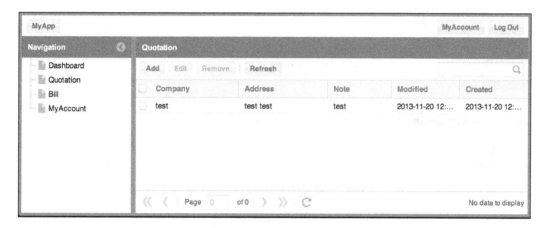

After clicking on the **Add** button, you'll see the following screenshot:

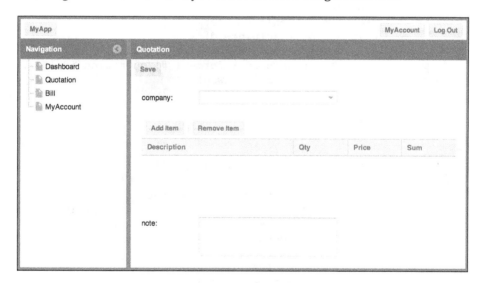

Let's implement the `add new` function. CT is the place to develop it. It will happen
with `ct/quotation/app_edit.htm`.

First implement the **Save** button. Acquire the **Save** button with the component query as `'myapp-quotation-edit button[action=save]'` and set up the `click` event. The handler name is `onSave`.

Let's create it in a way that when the **Save** button is pressed, the event handler is registered in the `MyApp.controller.quotation.Edit` class (source file: `05_loading_the_grid_and_implementing_toolbar_buttons/app/controller/quotation/Edit.js`).

```
me.control({
    ....
    'myapp-quotation-edit button[action=save]': {
        'click': me.onSave
    }
});
```

We'll also implement the inside of the handler.

```
    ...
onSave: function() {
    var me     = this,
        p       = me.getEditView(),
        form    = p.getForm(),
        format  = Ext.String.format,
        id;
    p.setLoading();
    form.submit({
        success: function(form, action) {
            if(action.result.newid) {
                p.fireEvent('myapp-list-reload');
                location.href = format('#!/quotation/id={0}',
                action.result.newid);
                return;
            }
            p.setLoading(false);
            form.load({
                params: {
                    id: form.getValues()['id']
                },
                success: function(form, ret) {
                    p.fireEvent('myapp-loadform', p, ret);
                    p.fireEvent('myapp-undirty');
                    p.setLoading(false);
                },
                failure: function() {
                    p.setLoading(false);
                }
            });
        },
```

```
        failure: function(form, action) {
            p.setLoading(false);
        }
    });
},
```

Call the `submit` method for the form in `onSave` and transmit the position to the server side. Next comes server-side implementation.

The Ext Direct module has already been prepared, and the processing will be implemented there. You probably remember the method is called `writeForm`.

Here we'll implement the `writeForm` method. The code is very long, so again please refer to the source file (source file: `05_loading_the_grid_and_implementing_toolbar_buttons/php/classes/MyAppQuotation.php`).

With this method the received position is being stored in the `Quotation` table. We are already storing certain data in quotations, so write the data in a different table as well.

In order to guarantee that correct data is written, you need to use `Transaction`, so use `begin`, `rollback`, and `commit`. In MySQL, if we use `last_insert_id()`, we can acquire the previous ID that we wrote.

Use this and set up the parent for quotations. In CT, even if we perform the screen transfer process, it will remain as it is when it loads. It should look like the following URL.

```
<hostname>/ct/quotation/app_edit.html#!/quotation/id=XX
```

Now, if we run it in the application, the URL will change in the following way:

```
<hostname>/#!/quotation/id=XX
```

With that present status, start reading again. The specific data you used has disappeared and just one item is being displayed. This is the reason why we stopped at creating mock data in *Chapter 3, Data Input*.

We need to expand the `readForm` method, which is at the root of all of this. However, before that, in order to have the ID cross over for the `readForm` argument, first amend the `config.php` file.

We will change the argument in the `readForm` method of the `MyAppQuotation` class from 0 to 1 (source file: `05_loading_the_grid_and_implementing_toolbar_buttons/php/config.php`).

Once we have amended the `config.php` file, we will amend the `readForm` method so it can actually receive arguments (source file: `05_loading_the_grid_and_implementing_toolbar_buttons/php/classes/MyAppQuotation.php`).

```php
<?php
class MyAppQuotation {
  public function readForm($id) {
```

Set the `$id` argument in the `readForm` method to identify the target. Now, this time, do the same at the JavaScript side (source file: `05_loading_the_grid_and_implementing_toolbar_buttons/app/view/quotation/Edit.js`).

```
Ext.define('MyApp.view.quotation.Edit', {
    ....
    paramOrder: ['id'],
    ....
```

With this, the ID can transmit to the server side. Now let's implement the main `readForm` method.

This is the implementation of the inside of the `readForm` method that we amended the arguments to earlier. Because the source code is very long, please refer to the source file for the code (source file: `05_loading_the_grid_and_implementing_toolbar_buttons/php/classes/MyAppQuotation.php`).

After you have read the data from the `Quotation` table with the ID that you set up, acquire the data from the `Quotations` table, convert the array into JSON, and save it.

Customer names are dependent on the `MyApp.store.Customer` data. If you want to match it with the customer table in the database, please customize it to read the data via `direct` to the store. Pretty simple!

Managing toolbar buttons depending on the grid selection's status

Now reading and writing of the data is complete. There's only the `Add` function in the list, so at present we can only add new information. Let's create it so we can click on the **Edit** and **Remove** buttons. After this we can implement the various functions. This implementation happens in `ct/quotation/app_list.html`.

Let's control the events when items are selected and deselected in the list. Also, we'll implement it so when you double-click on an item, it will perform in the same way as when you click on the **Edit** button.

We'll add the following event handler to the process occurring in the control of the init method of the MyApp.controller.quotation.List class (source file: 06_management_toolbar_buttons_depend_on_grid_selection_status/app/controller/quotation/List.js).

```
....
'myapp-quotation-list': {
    'myapp-show': me.onShow,
    'select': me.onSelect,
    'itemdblclick': me.onItemDblClick,
    'deselect': me.onDeselect
},
....
```

The following three are event handlers that will listen to specific events:

- select
- itemdblclick
- deselect

Let's go ahead and implement the various event handlers that will listen to the preceding three events. Next, we'll implement a handler to the previous step (source file: 06_management_toolbar_buttons_depend_on_grid_selection_status/app/controller/quotation/List.js).

onSelect
```
onSelect: function() {
    var me = this,
        listView = me.getListView(),
        btnEdit = listView.down('button[action=edit]'),
        btnRemove = listView.down('button[action=remove]'),
        sm = listView.getSelectionModel(),
        cnt = sm.getCount();
    if(cnt === 1) {
        btnEdit.enable();
    } else {
        btnEdit.disable();
    }
    if(cnt > 0) {
        btnRemove.enable();
    } else {
        btnRemove.disable();
    }
},
```

onDeselect
```
onDeselect: function() {
    var me = this,
```

```
            listView    = me.getListView(),
            btnEdit     = listView.down('button[action=edit]'),
            btnRemove   = listView.down('button[action=remove]'),
            sm          = listView.getSelectionModel(),
            cnt         = sm.getCount();
    if(cnt === 1) {
        btnEdit.enable();
    } else {
        btnEdit.disable();
    }
    if(cnt > 0) {
        btnRemove.enable();
    } else {
        btnRemove.disable();
    }
}
```

Regarding selections, we'll only have the **Edit** button available when one item is selected. We'll make **Remove** available even when multiple items are selected. Both the **Edit** and **Remove** buttons will be unavailable when no items are selected.

onItemDblClick
```
onItemDblClick: function(p, record, item, index, e, eOpts) {
    var me          = this,
        listView    = me.getListView();
    listView.fireEvent('myapp-edit', record.data.id);
},
```

When double-clicked, the `myapp-edit` event will fire, and the selected item ID will be added to the argument.

Now all that remains is to implement the process for when the **Edit** and **Remove** buttons are pressed. The implementation of the **Edit** button happens in the following way:

onItemEdit
```
onItemEdit: function() {
    var me = this,
        listView = me.getListView(),
        sm = listView.getSelectionModel(),
        record = sm.getLastSelected();
    listView.fireEvent('myapp-edit', record.data.id);
},
```

The process is mostly the same as for onItemDblClick; however, the record object is not passed across by the argument, so acquire the record object that has been selected from SelectionModel.

So, if you implement the myapp-edit event handler, it's going to start to feel like the end. The myapp-edit event handler will be implemented by the MyApp.controller. quotation.Quotation controller (source file: 06_management_toolbar_buttons_ depend_on_grid_selection_status/app/controller/quotation/Quotation.js).

```
Ext.define('MyApp.controller.quotation.Quotation', {
    ....
    init: function() {
        var me = this,
            format = Ext.String.format;
        me.control({
            'myapp-quotation-list': {
                'myapp-add': function() {
                    location.href = format('#!/{0}/new',
                    me.screenName);
                },
                'myapp-edit': function(itemid) {
                    var query = this.requestParams.q;
                    if(query) {
                        location.href = format('#!/{0}/id={1}/q={2}',
                        me.screenName, itemid, query);
                    } else {
                        location.href = format('#!/{0}/id={1}',
                        me.screenName, itemid);
                    }
                }
            }
        }
    });
```

Looking at the requestParams property, we're trying to decide whether or not there is a query. However, this will be configured in the SearchField, which will be implemented later.

Change one line of the onShow method implementation in the following way:

```
me.requestParams = params = o;
```

With this, if you double-click or if you click on the **Edit** button, the URL will change. If you check the whole application, when you click on the **Edit** button, you can check the particular screen where data is being read.

Next, implement the **Delete** button (source file: `06_management_toolbar_buttons_depend_on_grid_selection_status/app/controller/quotation/List.js`).

```
onItemRemove: function() {
    var me         = this,
        listView   = me.getListView(),
        sm         = listView.getSelectionModel(),
        records    = sm.getSelection();
    Ext.MessageBox.confirm(
        'Remove Confirm',
        'May I delete that?',
        function(ret) {
            if(ret === 'yes') {
                listView.fireEvent('myapp-remove', records);
            }
        }
    );
},
```

In terms of structure, it's the same as the **Edit** button. It fires the `myapp-remove` event. In the same way, `myapp-remove` implements the event handler in `MyApp.controller.quotation.Quotation` (source file: `06_management_toolbar_buttons_depend_on_grid_selection_status/app/controller/quotation/Quotation.js`).

```
onRemove: function(records) {
    var me = this,
        format = Ext.String.format,
        listView = me.getListView(),
        ids = [];
    if(!Ext.isArray(records)) {
        records = [records];
    }
    Ext.iterate(records, function(r) {
        if(r.get) {
            ids.push(r.get('id'));
        } else {
            ids.push(r);
        }
    });
    listView.mask();
    MyAppQuotation.removeItems(ids, function() {
        me.getController(
            format(
                '{0}.List',
                me.screenName.split('-').join('.')
            )
        ).onStoreRefresh();
```

```
        listView.unmask();
    });
}
```

We are calling the `direct` function called `MyAppQuotation.removeItems`. We haven't implemented this method yet. It's for deleting items, so let's do it quickly.

We're going to add a new `removeItems` (`len:1`) method to the `MyAppQuotation` class (source file: `06_management_toolbar_buttons_depend_on_grid_selection_status/php/config.php`).

Let's implement the method we added previously. The code is very long, so please refer to the source files (source file: `06_management_toolbar_buttons_depend_on_grid_selection_status/php/classes/MyAppQuotation.php`).

This method is not for physical deletion but for logic deletion after renewing the status of the UPDATE text. After you have finished with this process, we would call `onStoreRefresh` from the client side; however, it still hasn't been implemented so let's implement it (source file: `06_management_toolbar_buttons_depend_on_grid_selection_status/app/controller/quotation/List.js`).

```
Ext.define('MyApp.controller.quotation.List', {
    ....
    onStoreRefresh: function() {     },
    ....
```

This is actually only executing the toolbar renewal process, but it won't run without the store being configured on the toolbar. So for a final touch, let's set up the store in the toolbar (source file: `06_management_toolbar_buttons_depend_on_grid_selection_status/app/view/quotation/List.js`).

```
Ext.define('MyApp.view.quotation.List', {
    ....
    initComponent: function() {
        ....
        Ext.apply(me, {
            ....
            bbar: {
                xtype       : 'pagingtoolbar',
                store       : store,
                displayInfo : true
            }
        ....
```

Now, it will automatically execute the reload process after the deletion process. With this we have implemented the process from start to finish. It was a rather complicated and long journey! For `Bill`, please implement it in the same way as with `Quotation`, as the process to set it up is mostly the same.

Using a search trigger field and a relation URL hash

Finally, let's implement the `SearchField` in the top-right corner of the screen. Actually, it is already implemented on the client side.

When we are calling `getGrid` with the `cond` argument, the search criteria is being transmitted. That is to say, we just need to implement on the server side. Let's amend this quickly.

This just shows a section that has been amended. To see the whole section of the source code, please refer to the source files (source file: `07_using_search_trigger_field_and_relation_url_hash/php/classes/MyAppQuotation.php`).

```
    . . . .
        'ON',
        '    customers.id = quotation.customer',
        'WHERE',
        '    quotation.status = 1'
    ));
    $query = explode(' ', @$cond->query);
    foreach($query as $q) {
        if($q != '') {
            $sql .= ' ' . implode(" \n ", array(
                'AND (',
                '    customers.name like \'%' . $q . '%\'',
                '    OR',
                '    customers.addr1 like \'%' . $q . '%\'',
                '    OR',
                '    customers.`addr2` like \'%' . $q . '%\'',
                '    OR',
                '    quotation.`note` like \'%' . $q . '%\'',
                ')'
            ));
        }
    }
    . . . .
```

With `$cond`, the following parameters are sent:

- query
- page
- start
- limit

The character string you inputted in the `SearchField` is being stored in the query. Afterwards, you just need to take that character string and add new conditions to SQL.

We won't implement it here, but by applying `page`, `start`, and `limit` to SQL, the paging process will start.

Again, to set the display order when you click on the column, the sort functionality is added and sent. Using that data, if we add ORDER BY, you can adjust the order.

So in order to get closer to the real application, have a go at the implementation.

Summary

Until now we created the data structure, the application architecture, and implemented data sending and data receiving methods. But currently we can only see the data in a grid.

It's not hard to imagine a situation where a manager in a company wants to see this data in a chart for a report or a presentation. So in the next chapter we'll learn how to design various types of visual charts.

5
Reporting

In this chapter we will create the report and display it with four different types of graphs on the dashboard.

You will learn to:

- Create a pie chart to display the quotation and bill data
- Create a bar chart to display the data of the customer
- Create a line chart to display the quotation and bill data by month
- Create a radar chart for monetary amounts
- Display each chart inside a panel
- Layout four panels in the dashboard

Creating charts on dashboard

First create four empty panels and make it so that the **component test** (CT) can display them. These panels are for a pie chart, bar chart, line chart, and a radar chart. This process is very simple and now you should have four empty panels prepared.

To create each chart class as before, we will copy a different `view.html` and create a new HTML, modify the title and the JavaScript file.

Pie chart for CT

Let's create the class name with `MyApp.view.dashboard.Pie`. Please see the following source files for the code:

- `01_making_charts_on_dashboard/ct/dashboard/pie_view.html`

- `01_making_charts_on_dashboard/ct/dashboard/pie_view.js`

```
...
Ext.onReady(function() {
    Ext.create('MyApp.view.dashboard.Pie', {
        width: 800,
        height: 600,
        renderTo: Ext.getBody()
    });
});
...
```

We'll now implement the class specified in the previous code (source file: `01_making_charts_on_dashboard/app/view/dashboard/Pie.js`).

```
Ext.define('MyApp.view.dashboard.Pie', {
    extend: 'Ext.panel.Panel',
    alias : 'widget.myapp-dashboard-pie',
    title: 'Pie Chart'
});
```

Bar chart for CT

The content is the same as for the bar chart. Let's create the class name with `MyApp.view.dashboard.Bar`. Please see the following source files for the code:

- `01_making_charts_on_dashboard/ct/dashboard/bar_view.html`

- `01_making_charts_on_dashboard/ct/dashboard/bar_view.js`

- `01_making_charts_on_dashboard/app/view/dashboard/Bar.js`

```
Ext.define('MyApp.view.dashboard.Bar', {
    extend: 'Ext.panel.Panel',
    alias : 'widget.myapp-dashboard-bar',
    title: 'Bar Chart'
});
```

Line chart for CT

The same as with a pie chart and bar chart, let's create the class name with `MyApp.view.dashboard.Line`. Please see the following source files for the code:

- `01_making_charts_on_dashboard/ct/dashboard/line_view.html`
- `01_making_charts_on_dashboard/ct/dashboard/line_view.js`
- `01_making_charts_on_dashboard/app/view/dashboard/Line.js`

```
Ext.define('MyApp.view.dashboard.Line', {
    extend: 'Ext.panel.Panel',
    alias : 'widget.myapp-dashboard-line',
    title: 'Line Chart'
});
```

Radar chart for CT

In the same way as the other charts, let's create the class name with `MyApp.view.dashboard.Radar`. Please see the following source files for the code:

- `01_making_charts_on_dashboard/ct/dashboard/radar_view.html`
- `01_making_charts_on_dashboard/ct/dashboard/radar_view.js`
- `01_making_charts_on_dashboard/app/view/dashboard/Radar.js`

```
Ext.define('MyApp.view.dashboard.Radar', {
    extend: 'Ext.panel.Panel',
    alias : 'widget.myapp-dashboard-radar',
    title: 'Radar Chart'
});
```

Layout to dashboard

So, let's arrange these four panels onto the dashboard (source file: `02_layout_to_dashboard/app/view/dashboard/DashBoard.js`).

```
Ext.define('MyApp.view.dashboard.DashBoard', {

    requires: [
        'MyApp.view.dashboard.Pie',
        'MyApp.view.dashboard.Bar',
        'MyApp.view.dashboard.Line',
        'MyApp.view.dashboard.Radar'
    ],
    title: 'Dashboard',
    layout: {
        type: 'hbox',
```

```
            pack: 'start',
            align: 'stretch'
        },
    items: [{
            xtype: 'container',
            flex: 1,
            padding: '20 10 20 20',
            layout: {
                type: 'vbox',
                pack: 'start',
                align: 'stretch'
            },
            items: [{
                flex: 1,
                padding: '0 0 10 0',
                xtype: 'myapp-dashboard-pie'
            }, {
                flex: 1,
                padding: '10 0 0 0',
                xtype: 'myapp-dashboard-bar'
            }]
        }, {
            xtype: 'container',
            flex: 1,
            padding: '20 20 20 10',
            layout: {
                type: 'vbox',
                pack: 'start',
                align: 'stretch'
            },
            items: [{
                flex: 1,
                padding: '0 0 10 0',
                xtype: 'myapp-dashboard-line'
            }, {
                flex: 1,
                padding: '10 0 0 0',
                xtype: 'myapp-dashboard-radar'
            }]
        }]
    }]
});
```

Now, in the `requires` parameter on the dashboard panel, set up the four panels you made earlier. You can specify the `xtype` in items by doing this.

Next comes the layout part. In the `hbox` layout divide the top and bottom equally into two equal areas, then in each area divide the left and right with the `vbox` layout.

An important point is that `container` is being specified by the `xtype`. Having seen a variety of Ext JS code, in this case a lot of code doesn't specify the `xtype`. In such a case, `panel` will be specified as the initial value.

If you just want to execute the layout, you should specify the `container` parameter. If you don't do that and use `panel`, an unnecessary DOM will be created just for carrying out the layout and will badly affect the performance.

Now that you have successfully divided the dashboard into four parts, in order to adjust the appearance, make the adjustments to the padding. Of course, it's okay to do this directly with CSS.

In each of the four areas, set up the chart panels with `xtype`.

Hopefully your database is starting to take shape. Let's continue and implement the various charts.

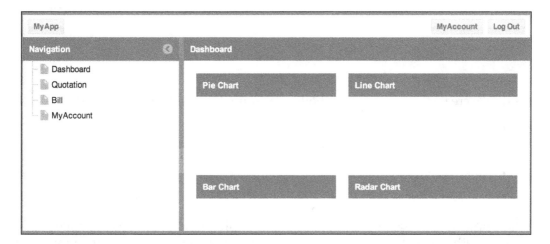

Creating a pie chart

First, we made the CT for display purposes, but now let's create the CT to make it run.

We will use the `Direct` function, so let's prepare that as well. In reality we've done this already.

Duplicate a different `app.html` and change the JavaScript file like we have done before. Please see the source file for the code: `03_making_a_pie_chart/ct/dashboard/pie_app.html`.

Implementing the Direct function

Next, prepare the `Direct` function to read the data.

First, it's the `config.php` file that defines the API. Let's gather them together and implement the four graphs (source file: `04_implement_direct_function/php/config.php`).

```
. . . .
'MyAppDashBoard'=>array(
    'methods'=>array(
        'getPieData'=>array(
            'len'=>0
        ),
        'getBarData'=>array(
            'len'=>0
        ),
        'getLineData'=>array(
            'len'=>0
        ),
        'getRadarData'=>array(
            'len'=>0
        )
    )
)
. . . .
```

Next, let's create the following methods to acquire data for the various charts:

- `getPieData`
- `getBarData`
- `getLineData`
- `getRadarData`

First, implement the `getPieData` method for the pie chart. We'll implement the `Direct` method to get the data for the pie chart. Please see the actual content for the source code (source file: `04_implement_direct_function/php/classes/MyAppDashBoard.php`).

This is acquiring valid quotation and bill data items. With the data to be sent back to the client, set the array in items and set up the various names and data in a key array. You will now combine the definitions in the next model.

Preparing the store for the pie chart

Charts need a store, so let's define the store and model (source file: `05_prepare_ the_store_for_the_pie_chart/app/model/ Pie.js`).

We'll create the `MyApp.model.Pie` class that has the `name` and `data` fields. Connect this with the data you set with the return value of the `Direct` function. If you increased the number of fields inside the model you just defined, make sure to amend the return field values, otherwise it won't be applied to the chart, so be careful. We'll use the model we made in the previous step and implement the store (source file: `05_prepare_the_store_for_the_pie_chart/app/model/ Pie.js`).

```
Ext.define('MyApp.store.Pie', {
    extend: 'Ext.data.Store',
    storeId: 'DashboardPie',
    model: 'MyApp.model.Pie',
    proxy: {
        type: 'direct',
        directFn: 'MyAppDashboard.getPieData',
        reader: {
            type: 'json',
            root: 'items'
        }
    }
})
```

Then, define the store using the model we made and set up the `Direct` function we made earlier in the proxy.

Creating the View

We have now prepared the presentation data. Now, let's quickly create the view to display it (source file: `06_making_the_view/app/view/dashboard/Pie.js`).

```
Ext.define('MyApp.view.dashboard.Pie', {
    extend: 'Ext.panel.Panel',
    alias : 'widget.myapp-dashboard-pie',
    title: 'Pie Chart',
    layout: 'fit',
    requires: [
        'Ext.chart.Chart',
        'MyApp.store.Pie'
    ],
    initComponent: function() {
        var me = this, store;
        store = Ext.create('MyApp.store.Pie');
```

```
        Ext.apply(me, {
            items: [{
                xtype: 'chart',
                store: store,
                series: [{
                    type: 'pie',
                    field: 'data',
                    showInLegend: true,
                label: {
                    field: 'name',
                    display: 'rotate',
                    contrast: true,
                    font: '18px Arial'
                }
            }]
            }]
        });
        me.callParent(arguments);
    }
});
```

Implementing the controller

With the previous code, data is not being read by the store and nothing is being displayed.

In the same way that reading was performed with onShow, let's implement the controller (source file: 06_making_the_view/app/controller/DashBoard.js):

```
Ext.define('MyApp.controller.dashboard.DashBoard', {
    extend: 'MyApp.controller.Abstract',
    screenName: 'dashboard',
    init: function() {
        var me = this;
        me.control({
            'myapp-dashboard': {
                'myapp-show': me.onShow,
                'myapp-hide': me.onHide
            }
        });
    },
    onShow: function(p) {
        p.down('myapp-dashboard-pie chart').store.load();
    },
    onHide: function() {
    }
});
```

With the charts we create from now on, as we create them it would be good to add the reading process to onShow. Let's take a look at our pie chart which appears as follows:

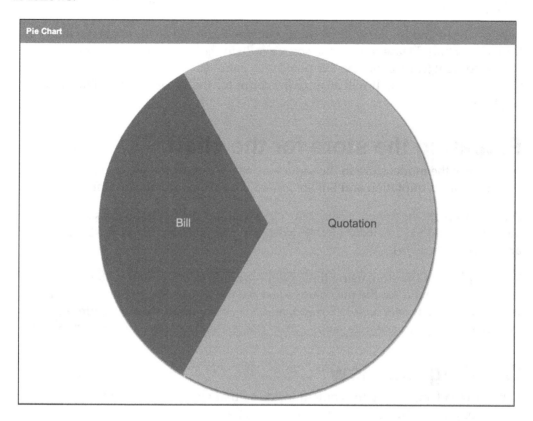

Creating a bar chart

In the same way as with the pie chart, first prepare the CT. Again in the same way as creating the pie chart, let's change the JavaScript file and create the bar chart HTML (source file: 07_making_a_bar_chart/ct/dashboard/bar_app.html).

Apart from the created class name (MyApp.view.dashboard.Bar), the JavaScript file here is the same as the pie chart (source file: 07_making_a_bar_chart/ct/dashboard/bar_app.js).

Implementing the Direct function

Now, it's the `Direct` function. As the definition is already made in `config.php`, I will not repeat it here.

Let's go ahead and implement the `Direct` method (`getBarData`) to get the data for the bar chart. Please refer to the source code in the source file if you want to see the content (source file: `08_implement_direct_function/php/classes/ MyAppDashBoard.php`). It will acquire the count for the levels of quotations or bills created for each client.

Preparing the store for the chart

Next comes the model store in the same way as we did for the pie chart. The name is the client name; quotation and bill are where the various counts are stored.

We'll now create the `MyApp.model.Bar` class that has the fields, such as `name`, `quotation`, and `bill` (source file: `09_prepare_the_store_for_the_pie_chart/ app/model/ Bar.js`).

We'll implement the store using the model we made in the previous step. It is the same way as we did for the pie chart so just see the source file if you need reference. Be careful as the model `name`, `StoreId`, and `Direct` method titles are different (source file: `09_prepare_the_store_for_the_pie_chart/app/store/ Bar.js`).

Creating the view

Let's go ahead and define the content inside so that we can display it (source file: `10_making_the_view/app/view/dashboard/Bar.js`):

```
Ext.define('MyApp.view.dashboard.Bar', {
    extend: 'Ext.panel.Panel',
    alias : 'widget.myapp-dashboard-bar',
    title: 'Bar Chart',
    layout: 'fit',
    requires: [
        'Ext.chart.Chart',
        'MyApp.store.Bar'
    ],
    initComponent: function() {
        var me = this, store;
        store = Ext.create('MyApp.store.Bar');
        Ext.apply(me, {
            items: [{
                xtype: 'chart',
                store: store,
                axes: [{
```

```
                        type: 'Numeric',
                        position: 'bottom',
                        fields: ['quotation', 'bill'],
                        title: 'Document Count',
                        grid: true,
                        minimum: 0
                    }, {
                        type: 'Category',
                        position: 'left',
                        fields: ['name'],
                        title: 'Customers'
                    }],
                    series: [{
                        type: 'bar',
                        axis: 'bottom',
                        highlight: true,
                        tips: {
                            trackMouse: true,
                            width: 140,
                            height: 28,
                            renderer: function(storeItem, item) {
                                var tail = '';
                                if(storeItem.get(item.yField) > 1) {
                                    tail = 's';
                                }
                                this.setTitle([
                                    storeItem.get('name'),
                                    ': ',
                                    storeItem.get(item.yField),
                                    ' ',
                                    item.yField,
                                ].join(''));
                            }
                        },
                        label: {
                            display: 'insideEnd',
                            field: 'quotation',
                            renderer: Ext.util.Format.numberRenderer('0'),
                            orientation: 'horizontal',
                            color: '#333',
                            'text-anchor': 'middle'
                        },
                        xField: 'name',
                        yField: ['quotation', 'bill']
                    }]
                }]
            });
        me.callParent(arguments);
    }
});
```

Implementing the controller

Like what we did with onShow, I'll put this implementation in a postscript
(source file: 11_making_the_view/app/controller/DashBoard.js).

```
....
onShow: function(p) {
    p.down('myapp-dashboard-pie chart').store.load();
    p.down('myapp-dashboard-bar chart').store.load();
},
....
```

Let's take a look at our bar chart which appears as follows:

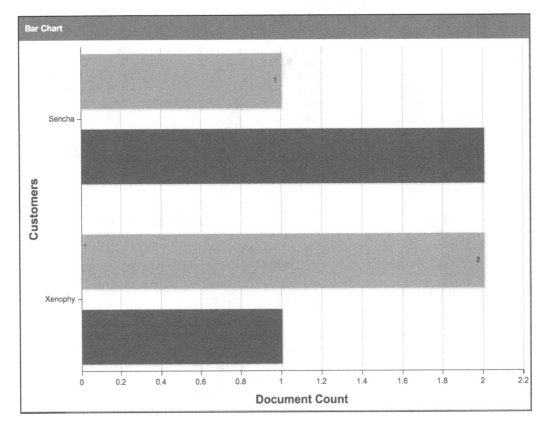

Creating a line chart

As before, let's set out by creating the CT. In the same way as for the pie chart, change the JavaScript file to be read and create the line chart HTML (source file: `12_making_a_line_chart/ct/dashboard/line_app.html`).

In this JavaScript file, everything is the same as the pie chart apart from the create class name: `MyApp.view.dashboard.Line` (source file: `12_making_a_line_chart/ct/dashboard/line_app.js`).

Implementing the Direct function

In the same way, implement the `Direct` function. Let's implement the `Direct` method (`getLineData`) to acquire data in the same way as we did for the bar chart. Please refer to the source file if you want to see the source code (source file: `13_implement_direct_function/php/classes/ MyAppDashBoard.php`).

Preparing the store for the chart

Create the model store in a similar way. We'll create the `MyApp.model.Line` class that has the fields `name`, `quotation`, and `bill` (source file: `14_prepare_the_store_for_the_pie_chart/app/model/ Line.js`).

We'll now implement the store using the model we made in the previous step. The details are the same as in the pie chart. Refer to the following source file for the code. Again, the model `name`, `StoreId`, and `Direct` method titles have changed so take note of this (source file: `14_prepare_the_store_for_the_pie_chart/app/store/ Line.js`).

Creating the view

Let's make the `quotation` and `bill` variables to display per month. With the `Direct` function, at most it can receive output of 12 months, and in case that the data doesn't exist, the number of months will decrease (source file: `15_making_the_view/app/view/dashboard/Line.js`).

```
Ext.define('MyApp.view.dashboard.Line', {
    extend: 'Ext.panel.Panel',
    alias : 'widget.myapp-dashboard-line',
    title: 'Line Chart',
    layout: 'fit',
    requires: [
        'MyApp.store.Line'
    ],
    initComponent: function() {
```

```
            var me = this, store;
            store = Ext.create('MyApp.store.Line');
            Ext.apply(me, {
                items: [{
                    xtype: 'chart',
                    store: store,
                    legend: {
                        position: 'right'
                    },
                    axes: [{
                        type: 'Numeric',
                        minimum: 0,
                        position: 'left',
                        fields: ['quotation', 'bill'],
                        title: 'Documents',
                        minorTickSteps: 1
                    }, {
                        type: 'Category',
                        position: 'bottom',
                        fields: ['mon'],
                        title: 'Month of the Year'
                    }],
                    series: [{
                        type: 'line',
                        highlight: {
                            size: 7,
                            radius: 7
                        },
                        axis: 'left',
                        xField: 'mon',
                        yField: 'quotation'
                    }, {
                        type: 'line',
                        highlight: {
                            size: 7,
                            radius: 7
                        },
                        axis: 'left',
                        xField: 'mon',
                        yField: 'bill'
                    }]
                }]
            });
            me.callParent(arguments);
        }
    });
```

Implementing the controller

As it is the same process, I will add a postscript about the command to read the controller store (source file: `16_making_the_view/app/controller/DashBoard.js`).

```
....
onShow: function(p) {
    p.down('myapp-dashboard-pie chart').store.load();
    p.down('myapp-dashboard-bar chart').store.load();
    p.down('myapp-dashboard-line chart').store.load();
},
....
```

Let's take a look at our line chart which appears as follows:

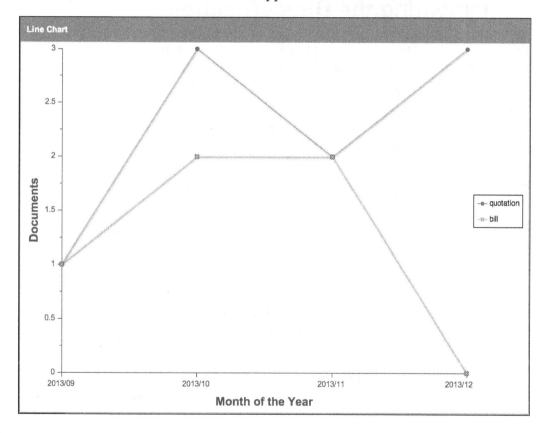

Creating a radar chart

Now, let's make the final CT.

In the same way as the pie chart, change the JavaScript file to be read and create the radar chart HTML (source file: `17_making_a_radar_chart/ct/dashboard/radar_app.html`).

Again, everything is the same as the pie chart in this JavaScript file apart from the create class name: `MyApp.view.dashboard.Radar` (source file: `17_making_a_radar_chart/ct/dashboard/radar_app.js`).

Implementing the Direct function

As the title says, let's implement the `Direct` function. As before, we'll implement the `Direct` method (`getRadarData`) to acquire the data for the radar chart. Please refer to the following source file for details (source file: `18_implement_direct_function/php/classes/ MyAppDashBoard.php`).

You've guessed it, the process is exactly the same as the `getLineData`. So, there's no need to implement it unnecessarily, but if you want to display different data on the radar chart, please amend this method.

Preparing the store for the chart

Let's prepare the store. We'll create the `MyApp.model.Radar` class that has the `name`, `quotation`, and `bill` fields (source file: `19_prepare_the_store_for_the_pie_chart/app/model/ Radar.js`).

Again, we'll implement the store with the model we made in the previous step. The details are the same as for the pie chart, and again be careful because the model `name`, `StoreId`, and `Direct` method titles are different (source file: `19_prepare_the_store_for_the_pie_chart/app/store/ Radar.js`).

Creating the view

Next, we will create the view (source file: `20_making_the_view/app/view/dashboard/Radar.js`):

```
Ext.define('MyApp.view.dashboard.Radar', {
    extend: 'Ext.panel.Panel',
    alias : 'widget.myapp-dashboard-radar',
    title: 'Radar Chart',
    layout: 'fit',
```

```
requires: [
    'MyApp.store.Radar'
],
initComponent: function() {
    var me = this, store;
    store = Ext.create('MyApp.store.Radar');
    Ext.apply(me, {
        items: [{
            xtype: 'chart',
            store: store,
            insetPadding: 20,
            legend: {
                position: 'right'
            },
            axes: [{
                type: 'Radial',
                position: 'radial',
                label: {
                    display: true
                }
            }],
            series: [{
                type: 'radar',
                xField: 'mon',
                yField: 'quotation',
                showInLegend: true,
                showMarkers: true,
                markerConfig: {
                    radius: 5,
                    size: 5
                },
                style: {
                    'stroke-width': 2,
                    fill: 'none'
                }
            },{
                type: 'radar',
                xField: 'mon',
                yField: 'bill',
                showInLegend: true,
                showMarkers: true,
                markerConfig: {
                    radius: 5,
                    size: 5
                },
                style: {
                    'stroke-width': 2,
                    fill: 'none'
                }
```

```
            }]
        }]
    });
    me.callParent(arguments);
}
});
```

Implementing the controller

Postscript the store's data reading settings in `onShow` (source file: `21_making_the_view/app/controller/DashBoard.js`).

```
....
onShow: function(p) {
    p.down('myapp-dashboard-pie chart').store.load();
    p.down('myapp-dashboard-bar chart').store.load();
    p.down('myapp-dashboard-line chart').store.load();
    p.down('myapp-dashboard-radar chart').store.load();
},
....
```

Finally, let's look at our radar chart which appears as follows:

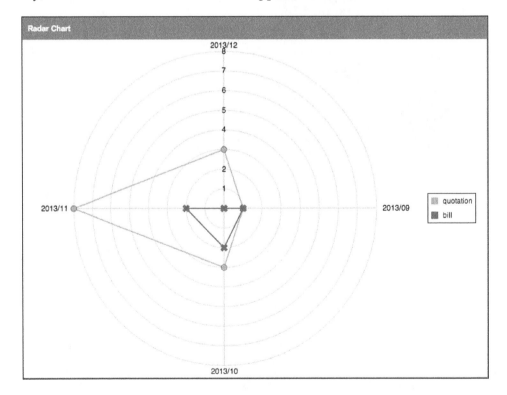

In the near future, the chart should look like the previous chart. However, in the current Ext JS 4.2.2-GPL Version, setting the store to a chart and acquiring the data from the server causes a bug that distorts the display of the lines and the labels. The bug has been confirmed as EXTJSIV-7778.

In the case of the previous chart, we managed to display it by taking the exact same response received from the server and setting it in the store's local data.

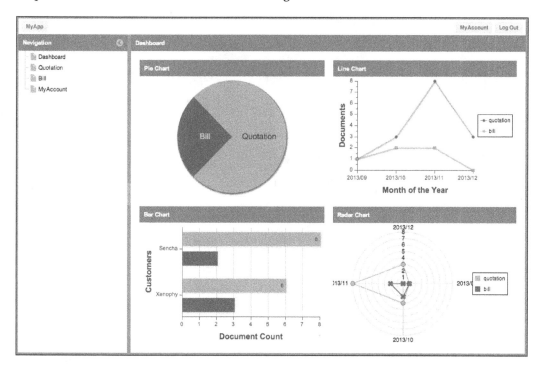

Summary

You must agree this is starting to look like an application!

The dashboard is the first screen you see right after logging in. Charts are extremely effective in order to visually check a large and complicated amount of data. If you keep adding panels as and when you feel it's needed, you'll increase its practicability. This sample will become a customizable base for you to use in future projects.

Now, in the next and final chapter we'll move on to data management.

6
Data Management

With the development we have done already, the application is really taking shape. We can input and see the data. Now if we customize the content according to the need, we'll have the finished application we were originally hoping for. In this final chapter, we will implement the data import/export to restore or backup the data. This time, the data we refer to is the Quotation and Bill data.

Designing Import and Export

Let's start by thinking about the Quotation table. Because Bill is mostly the same as Quotation, we'll just implement Quotation here. Try this implementation with Bill, as well by yourself. First, we'll add an Export and Import button in the Quotation list, so that it begins to function. Next, we'll make the file start downloading when the Export button is pressed. We'll add a new panel so that we can visually check the selected data that we are about to import. So let's go ahead and create this type of data import and export functions.

Data format

At first, when exporting, let's consider the data format in which it will be downloaded. This time, we're thinking of outputting in the **TSV format** instead of CSV or XML. TSV is easier for the developers to read and it's very simple to generate with JavaScript. The following list shows the order of output.

Quotation and Quotations are outputted in a single file. In the case of quotation, the order of output is as follows:

- quotation
- id
- status
- customer

- note
- modified
- created

In the case of quotations, the order of output is as follows:

- quotations
- id
- status
- parent
- description
- qty
- price
- sum
- modified
- created

For the very first item, enter the table name, this will let you output multiple tables at the same time.

Creating the Import and Export views in Quotation

First, we'll add the button feature and modify the code for import and export (source file: 01_making_the_import_and_export_view_in_quotation/app/view/quotation/List.js):

```
Ext.define('MyApp.view.quotation.List', {
    ....
    initComponent: function() {
        ....
        Ext.apply(me, {
            tbar: [{
                ....
            }, '-', {
                text     : 'Import',
                action   : 'import'
            }, {
                text     : 'Export',
                action   : 'export'
            }, '-', {
                ....
```

You should now see the following form:

Next, implement the button's event handler (source file: `01_making_the_import_` `and_export_view_in_quotation/app/controller/quotation/List.js`):.

```
Ext.define('MyApp.controller.quotation.List', {
    ....
    init: function() {
        var me = this;
        me.control({
            ....
            'myapp-quotation-list button[action=import]': {
                'click': me.onImport
            },
            'myapp-quotation-list button[action=export]': {
                'click': me.onExport
            }
        });
    },
    onImport: function() {
        // import
    },
    onExport: function() {
        // export
    },
```

Detect the actions for `import` and `export` you set up in the `button` feature, and then assign `onImport` and `onExport` to the various click events. Of course, we will make `onImport` and `onExport` from scratch.

Preparing the server side for export

In order to download the file, we will make the `quotation-export.php` file. The file can be installed anywhere, but this time we have positioned it in the document route where the `index.php` file is located.

The process to export the `Quotation` data will be implemented by PHP. It's a long one, so please refer to the source file for the code (source file: `02_preparing_the_` `server_side_for_export/quotation-export.php`).

Execute SQL and output it to match the data format we thought up earlier.

In order to change the filename to the second one, the filename that comes after the quotation will have the year, month, date, hour, minute, and second recorded. Then, it is downloaded with the `.tsv` file extension. Please check if you can download the file by entering the `quotation-export.php` URL directly.

Next, let's make this URL move when you press down the button we just made. (source file: `02_preparing_the_server_side_for_export/app/controller/quotation/List.js`):.

```
onExport: function() {
    location.href='quotation-export.php';
},
```

Creating a temporary view for import

Next, we will continue by implementing the import process. Like it was explained earlier, upload the data you will import and then implement it, so that you can import after you have visually checked it.

Let's make the `myapp-import` event fire when we press the `import` button, and implement it so that the panel shows to confirm the import data.

First, let's implement the listener. When this event happens, the URL will change to `#!/quotation/import` (source file: `03_making_a_temporary_view_for_import/app/controller/quotation/Quotation.js`):

```
Ext.define('MyApp.controller.quotation.Quotation', {
    ....
    init: function() {
        ....
        me.control({
            'myapp-quotation-list': {
                ....
                'myapp-import': function() {
                    location.href = '#!/quotation/import';
                }
            }
        });
```

Next, implement so that the event fires (source file: `03_making_a_temporary_view_for_import/app/controller/quotation/List.js`):

```
Ext.define('MyApp.controller.quotation.List', {
    ....
    init: function() {
        var me = this;
        me.control({
```

```
....
    'myapp-quotation-list button[action=import]': {
        'click': me.onImport
    },
    'myapp-quotation-list button[action=export]': {
        'click': me.onExport
    }
});
    },
    onImport: function() {
        var me        = this,
            listView  = me.getListView();

        listView.fireEvent('myapp-import');
    },
    ....
```

Implement the contents of the onImport method that we implemented earlier. From the List view object, fire the myapp-import event with fireEvent.

When this event happens, the URL will be changed. Next, modify onShow so that the panel for imports shows up (source file: 03_making_a_temporary_view_for_ import/app/controller/quotation/Quotation.js):

```
....
onShow: function(p) {
    var me = this,
        o = {},
        hash = location.hash,
        layout = p.getLayout(),
        listView = me.getListView(),
        editView = me.getEditView(),
        params;
    params = hash.substr(('#!/' + me.screenName + '/').length);
    if(params === 'new') {
        o.id = params;
    } else {
        if(!params || !Ext.isString(params)) {
            params = '';
        }
        params = params.split('/');
        Ext.iterate(params, function(text) {
            if(!text || !Ext.isString(text)) {
                text = '';
            }
            text = text.split('=');
            o[text[0]] = text[1];
        });
```

```
    }
    me.requestParams = params = o;

    if(params.hasOwnProperty('import')) {
        // Show Import
        layout.setActiveItem(2);
    } else if(params.id === 'new' || Number(params.id)) {
        // Show Edit
        layout.setActiveItem(1);
    } else {
        // Show List
        layout.setActiveItem(0);
    }
    // fire event 'myapp-show'
    layout.activeItem.fireEvent('myapp-show', layout.activeItem, p,
    params);
},
....
```

Parameter analysis is being performed by the process we made earlier. Using this process, if you have an `import` property, the `import` panel will be displayed.

We haven't made the main `import` panel. Here, we have just made a very simple panel so that it can be displayed for the time being (source file: `03_making_a_temporary_view_for_import/app/view/quotation/Import.js`):

```
Ext.define('MyApp.view.quotation.Import', {
    extend: 'MyApp.form.Panel',
    alias : 'widget.myapp-quotation-import',
    itemId: 'screen-quotation-import',
    initComponent: function() {
        var me = this;

        // TopToolbar
        Ext.apply(me, {
            tbar: [{
                text: 'Cancel',
                action: 'cancel'
            }, '-', {
                text: 'Upload',
                action: 'upload'
            }]
        });

        me.callParent(arguments);
    }
});
```

Add this panel (`app/view/quotation/Quotation.js`) to the `screen` panel item (source file: `03_making_a_temporary_view_for_import/app/view/quotation/Quotation.js`).

When you configure an item, you should specify the `xtype`. To do this, set up the class name it requires so that dynamic loading can take place.

In this state, execute the whole application. When you press the `import` button, the following panel will be displayed:

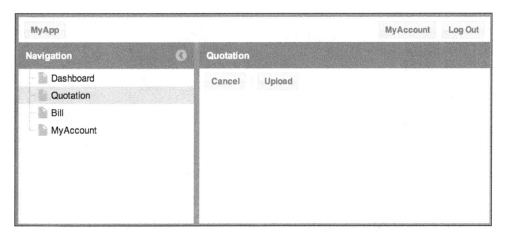

The `import` panel is still temporary, and the `grid` panel we implemented earlier is still not displayed; but we can check with the `onShow` event handler that it is changing properly.

Creating the CT view for import

We haven't created the CT that we usually would have made already. So, let's make the CT to display the temporary import panel we made earlier (source file: `04_making_the_ct_view_for_import/ct/quotation/view_import.html`).

For the HTML, there shouldn't be any problems if we duplicate a different HTML and amend the JavaScript file to be read in the same way (source file: `04_making_ the_ct_view_for_import/ct/quotation/view_import.js`):

```
...
Ext.onReady(function() {
    Ext.create('MyApp.store.Customer');
    Ext.create('MyApp.store.QuotationItem');
    Ext.create('MyApp.view.quotation.Quotation', {
        activeItem: 2,
```

```
        width: 800,
        height: 600,
        renderTo: Ext.getBody()
    });
});
```

Now, let's prepare a grid for this panel. After the upload is complete, it will receive the display data from JSON data. So, let's make a store with the `memory` proxy (source file: `04_making_the_ct_view_for_import/app/store/QuotationImport.js`):

```
Ext.define('MyApp.store.QuotationImport',{
    extend: 'Ext.data.Store',
    storeId:'QuotationImport',
    fields:['id', 'status', 'customer', 'note', 'modified', 'created'],
    data:{'items':[
    ]},
    proxy: {
        type: 'memory',
        reader: {
            type: 'json',
            root: 'items'
        }
    }
});
```

Also, use the following code to prepare a grid for this panel (source file: `04_making_the_ct_view_for_import/app/store/QuotationImportItems.js`):

```
Ext.define('MyApp.store.QuotationImportItems',{
    extend: 'Ext.data.Store',
    storeId:'QuotationImportItems',
    fields:[
        'id',
        'status',
        'parent',
        'description',
        'qty',
        'price',
        'sum',
        'modified',
        'created'
    ],
    data:{'items':[
    ]},
    proxy: {
        type: 'memory',
        reader: {
            type: 'json',
```

```
                   root: 'items'
               }
           }
       });
```

The reason we have created two `memory` proxies is because we will prepare one each for `Quotation` and `Quotations`, and then make two grids. Now, we are going to use this in `Grid`; but we will add the following code to make sure that it displays without any problems in CT (source file: 04_making_the_ct_view_for_import/ct/quotation/view_import.js).

To make sure that the two stores we made previously can use the `view_import.js` script in the CT directory, let's change it so that it can instantiate when it's initially launched.

Now, we'll quickly make the view. We'll remodel the temporary `Import` panel we made earlier (source file: 04_making_the_ct_view_for_import/app/view/quotation/Import.js):

```
Ext.define('MyApp.view.quotation.Import', {
    extend: 'MyApp.form.Panel',
    alias : 'widget.myapp-quotation-import',
    itemId: 'screen-quotation-import',
    initComponent: function() {
        var me = this,
            store = Ext.getStore('QuotationImport'),
            itemstore = Ext.getStore('QuotationImportItems');

        // Items
        Ext.apply(me, {
            layout: {
                type: 'border',
                padding: 5
            },
            items: [{
                region: 'north',
                xtype: 'grid',
                itemId: 'quotationgrid',
                split: true,
                title: 'Quotation',
                store: store,
                columns: [{
                    text: 'id',
                    dataIndex: 'id',
                    width: 50
                }, {
                    text: 'status',
                    dataIndex: 'status',
                    width : 50
```

```
        }, {
            text: 'customer',
            dataIndex: 'customer'
        }, {
            text: 'note',
            dataIndex: 'note',
            flex: 1
        }, {
            text: 'modified',
            dataIndex: 'modified'
        }, {
            text: 'created',
            dataIndex: 'created'
        }],
        flex:1
    }, {
        region: 'center',
        xtype: 'grid',
        title: 'Quotation Items',
        itemId: 'quotationitemsgrid',
        store: itemstore,
        columns: [{
            text: 'id',
            dataIndex: 'id',
            width: 50
        }, {
            text: 'status',
            dataIndex: 'status',
            width : 50
        }, {
            text: 'parent',
            dataIndex: 'parent',
            width : 50
        }, {
            text: 'description',
            dataIndex: 'description',
            flex: 1
        }, {
            text: 'qty',
            dataIndex: 'qty'
        }, {
            text: 'price',
            dataIndex: 'price'
        }, {
            text: 'sum',
            dataIndex: 'sum'
        }, {
            text: 'modified',
```

```
                    dataIndex: 'modified'
                }, {
                    text: 'created',
                    dataIndex: 'created'
                }],
                flex:1
            }]
        });

        // TopToolbar
        Ext.apply(me, {
            tbar: [{
                text: 'Cancel',
                action: 'cancel'
            }, '-', {
                text: 'Upload',
                action: 'upload'
            }]
        });

        me.callParent(arguments);
    }
});
```

As mentioned earlier, we will make two `grid` panels. This is for `Quotation` and `Quotations`. Again, the layout is a **border layout** and it specifies flex.

Users who have been using Ext JS for a long time might think this is strange; but with the current Ext JS, you can specify flex even in a border layout.

So, if you set up `flex:1` for both `north` and `center`, it will equally arrange the top and bottom of the form; and with `north` set up as `split:true`, the splitter can be displayed.

If you check the display, it will look like the following:

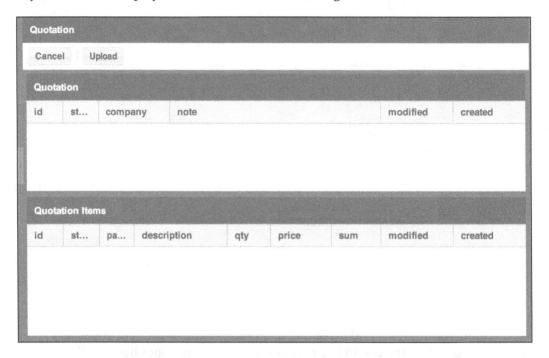

Creating Upload and Show Data in the grid

This time, upload the data you exported and let's display it in a grid. To do this, add a controller in `app.js`. You might have to jog your memory because it has been a while since the last time! (Source file: `05_making_upload_and_show_data_in_the_grid/app/Application.js`.):

```
    . . . .

    Ext.application({
        . . . .
        controllers: [
            . . . .
            'quotation.Import',
            . . . .
        ],
```

Now, we will make this controller (source file: `05_making_upload_and_show_data_in_the_grid/app/controller/quotation/Import.js`):

```
Ext.define('MyApp.controller.quotation.Import', {
    extend: 'MyApp.controller.Abstract',
    refs: [{
        ref: 'importView', selector: 'myapp-quotation-import'
    }],
    stores: [
        'QuotationImport',
        'QuotationImportItems'
    ],
    init: function() {
        var me = this;
        me.control({
            'myapp-quotation-import': {
                'myapp-show': me.onShow,
                'myapp-hide': me.onHide
            },
            'myapp-quotation-import [action=upload]': {
                'change': me.onUploaded
            }
        });
    },
    onShow: function(p, owner, params) {
    },
    onHide: function() {
    },
    onUploaded: function(fb, v) {
        var me = this,
            p = me.getImportView(),
            form = p.getForm(),
            importView = me.getImportView(),
            btnExecute = importView.down('button[action=execute]');

        p.setLoading();
        btnExecute.disable();
        form.submit({
            success: function(form, action) {
                Ext.getStore('QuotationImport').loadData(action.
                result.quotation.items);
                Ext.getStore('QuotationImportItems').loadData(action.
                result.quotations.items);
                p.setLoading(false);
                btnExecute.enable();
            }
        });
    }
});
```

Then, temporarily change the `upload` button (that we created previously) to `filefield` (source file: `05_making_upload_and_show_data_in_the_grid/app/view/quotation/Import.js`):

```
Ext.define('MyApp.view.quotation.Import', {
    extend: 'MyApp.form.Panel',
    alias : 'widget.myapp-quotation-import',
    itemId: 'screen-quotation-import',
    api: {
        submit   : 'MyAppQuotation.importData'
    },
    paramOrder: ['importfile'],
    initComponent: function() {
        ....

        // TopToolbar
        Ext.apply(me, {
            tbar: [{
                text: 'Cancel',
                action: 'cancel'
            }, '-', {
                xtype: 'filefield',
                name: 'importfile',
                buttonText: 'Upload',
                buttonOnly: true,
                hideLabel: true,
                action: 'upload'
            }]
        });

        me.callParent(arguments);
    }
});
```

Furthermore, add the API key in the config options and specify the `Direct` function in `submit`. This panel is a form panel. Upload the file using the `submit` method. Next, make the `Direct` function that we specified in `submit` (source file: `05_making_upload_and_show_data_in_the_grid/php/config.php`).

We'll add the following method to the `MyAppQuotation` class:

```
'importData'=>array(
    'len'=>2,
    'formHandler'=>true
)
```

We'll actually implement the method we added previously. It's too long to include in this text, so please refer to the source files for the code (source file: `05_making_upload_and_show_data_in_the_grid/php/classes/MyAppQuotation.php`).

Return the upload data again with JSON. If you are thinking of building an application, you should perform an input check because the user can input whatever information they like with a TSV file.

With the controller you implemented before, use the `loadData` method and read the data that was returned from the server side into the `MemoryStore` method.

Executing the Import data

Once you have displayed the read data in the grid and checked it, you can create a button to apply it to the database (source file: `06_execute_import_data /app/ view/quotation/Import.js`):

```
Ext.define('MyApp.view.quotation.Import', {
    ....
    initComponent: function() {
        ....

        // TopToolbar
        Ext.apply(me, {
            ....
            }, {
                text: 'Execute',
                disabled: true,
                action: 'execute'
            }]
        });

        me.callParent(arguments);
    }
});
```

Let's make it so that it is impossible to press the button in the initial state. It will enable the button once the previous data upload has been complete (source file: `06_execute_import_data /app/controller/quotation/Import.js`):

```
Ext.define('MyApp.controller.quotation.Import', {
    ....
    init: function() {
        var me = this;
        me.control({
            ....
            'myapp-quotation-import [action=execute]': {
                'click': me.onExecute
            }
        });
    },
    ....
```

```
        onExecute: function() {
            var data = {
                    quotation: [],
                    quotations: []
                },
                store = Ext.getStore('QuotationImport'),
                items = Ext.getStore('QuotationImportItems');

            Ext.iterate(store.data.items, function(item) {
                data.quotation.push(Ext.clone(item.data));
            });

            Ext.iterate(items.data.items, function(item) {
                data.quotations.push(Ext.clone(item.data));
            });

            MyAppQuotation.executeImport(data, function() {
                location.href = '#!/quotation';
            });
        }
    });
```

Now, we are calling the `executeImport` and `Direct` functions. That's right, we haven't made it yet. Let's make this and make it possible to receive data from the client side (source file: `06_execute_import_data /php/config.php`):

```
    ....
    'MyAppQuotation'=>array(
        'methods'=>array(

            ....
            'executeImport'=>array(
                'len'=>1
            )
        )
    ),
    ....
```

We'll implement the method we added to the `config.php` file. Again, this is too long to show here, so please refer to the source file (source file: `06_execute_import_data /php/classes/MyAppQuotation.php`).

When the data has been received, empty the inside of the database once with `Truncate` and insert the new data. Whether this is a good or bad way to do it will depend on the system you make.

Furthermore, if you look closely at the code, you'll know that error processing is not at a high level. If you are intending to make this at a commercial level, you will have to build up this area. Already, the implementation is complete. But finally, let's change the URL to `#!/quotation` to change it to a list display, and then finish.

Summary

We have motored through implementing the Export and Import data. There are still many points to cover, such as input checks and the error checks. But after learning this flow, I think you now have the base to customize this database in the way that you want.

Well done! You've made it to the end of the book!

Let's go over what you have achieved:

- You made the data structure
- You made the application architecture
- You made the input and output by using grids and fields on the browser
- You developed the application to obtain information using various charts
- You made the data export and import management features

Each feature is fundamental to an application of this kind. From now on, if you're thinking of creating something similar in your next project, please use this sample application as a base for your application. You only need to change a few points, and then you should be able to create a customized application very quickly.

Incorporating the architecture from this book into applications you have made, or are about to make, will simplify control and improve maintenance. It will also give you have high-level and versatile history management and let you add new screens with ease.

However, the sample application introduced in this book needed some extra features for actual real-world use. So we added some things here and there at the end of this chapter to brush up the application.

A list of the extra edited code files can be found in the sample code folder for this chapter. Please refer to this to see the final modifications we made to the application.

Also, we have included the comment // update code next to any modifications. Just search inside the code with that comment, and you should be able to see changes straight away.

Finally, remember that if you get lost, or if you hit a brick wall in one of your future projects, just take another look at this application and see if it can offer you some kind of solution.

I hope that you will be able to create some fantastic applications! Good luck and happy coding!

Index

component test, creating 21
controllers, adding 27-29
CT, into individual views 24
directory structure 18, 19
navigation section 30-32
options 19
production build, creating 23
project, creating 20, 21
testing 22, 23
View component 26
viewport 33, 34
views, creating 30
login page
creating 47

M

main controller 35
MyAccount controller 38
MyAccount form
creating 48, 50, 52
screen layout, making into card layout 48
myapp-add event handler 93
myapp-edit event 98
myapp-show event handler 76
MyApp.util.History class 39

N

navigation controller 35-37

O

onEditShow method 77
onImport method 129
onShow event handler 131
onShow method implementation 99

P

pie chart
controller, implementing 112, 113
creating 109
creating, for CT 106
Direct function, implementing 110

store, preparing 111
view, creating 111

Q

quotation and bill controller 38
Quotation controller
implementing 88-91
Quotation form
creating 52, 53
field component 55
grid component 55, 56
implementing 65-70
Store component 54
TopToolbar 56, 57
Quotation list
creating 82
Quotation model
creating 82, 83
Quotations table 9
Quotation table 9, 12
Quotation view
updating 84-88

R

radar chart
controller, implementing 122
creating 120
creating, for CT 107
Direct function, implementing 120
store, preparing 120
view, creating 120
read and write processes
implementing, with Ext Direct 72
readForm method 95
implementing 76
Remote Procedure Call (RPC) 43

S

SearchField
implementing 102, 103
Sencha Architect 51

T

toolbar buttons
   implementing 91-96
   managing 96-101
TSV format 125

U

user 7
User table 11

W

writeForm method
   implementing 76, 95

Thank you for buying
Ext JS Data-driven Application Design

About Packt Publishing

Packt, pronounced 'packed', published its first book "*Mastering phpMyAdmin for Effective MySQL Management*" in April 2004 and subsequently continued to specialize in publishing highly focused books on specific technologies and solutions.

Our books and publications share the experiences of your fellow IT professionals in adapting and customizing today's systems, applications, and frameworks. Our solution based books give you the knowledge and power to customize the software and technologies you're using to get the job done. Packt books are more specific and less general than the IT books you have seen in the past. Our unique business model allows us to bring you more focused information, giving you more of what you need to know, and less of what you don't.

Packt is a modern, yet unique publishing company, which focuses on producing quality, cutting-edge books for communities of developers, administrators, and newbies alike. For more information, please visit our website: www.packtpub.com.

About Packt Open Source

In 2010, Packt launched two new brands, Packt Open Source and Packt Enterprise, in order to continue its focus on specialization. This book is part of the Packt Open Source brand, home to books published on software built around Open Source licences, and offering information to anybody from advanced developers to budding web designers. The Open Source brand also runs Packt's Open Source Royalty Scheme, by which Packt gives a royalty to each Open Source project about whose software a book is sold.

Writing for Packt

We welcome all inquiries from people who are interested in authoring. Book proposals should be sent to author@packtpub.com. If your book idea is still at an early stage and you would like to discuss it first before writing a formal book proposal, contact us; one of our commissioning editors will get in touch with you.

We're not just looking for published authors; if you have strong technical skills but no writing experience, our experienced editors can help you develop a writing career, or simply get some additional reward for your expertise.

[PACKT] **open source**
PUBLISHING   community experience distilled

Ext JS 4 Plugin and Extension Development

ISBN: 978-1-78216-372-5   Paperback: 116 pages

A hands-on development of several Ext JS plugins and extensions

1. Easy-to-follow examples on Ext JS plugins and extensions

2. Step-by-step instructions on developing Ext JS plugins and extensions

3. Provides a walkthrough of several useful Ext JS libraries and communities

Ext JS 4 First Look

ISBN: 978-1-84951-666-2   Paperback: 340 pages

A practical guide including examples of the new features in Ext JS 4 and tips to migrate from Ext JS 3

1. Migrate your Ext JS 3 applications easily to Ext JS 4 based on the examples presented in this guide

2. Full of diagrams, illustrations, and step-by-step instructions to develop real word applications

3. Driven by examples and explanations of how things work

Please check **www.PacktPub.com** for information on our titles

Learning Ext JS 3.2

ISBN: 978-1-84951-120-9   Paperback: 432 pages

Build dynamic, desktop-style user interfaces for your data-driven web application using Ext JS

1. Learn to build consistent, attractive web interfaces with the framework components

2. Integrate your existing data and web services with Ext JS data support

3. Enhance your JavaScript skills by using Ext's DOM and AJAX helpers

4. Extend Ext JS through custom components

Instant Ext JS Starter

ISBN: 978-1-78216-610-8   Paperback: 56 pages

Find out what Ext JS actually is, what you can do with it, and why it's so great

1. Learn something new in an Instant! A short, fast, focused guide delivering immediate results.

2. Install and set up the environment with this quick Starter guide

3. Learn the basics of the framework and built-in utility functions

4. Use MVC architecture, components, and containers